Praise for *Fired Up*

"This book is a gift to any woman who is ready to rewrite her story."

—**DR. SHARON MALONE**, author of *Grown Women Talk: Your Guide to Getting and Staying Healthy*

"Shannon Watts not only looks inward with curiosity but also shines her light on other changemakers in a way that will remind you of your agency and strength."

—**DR. POOJA LAKSHMIN**, psychiatrist and author of *Real Self-Care: A Transformative Program for Redefining Wellness (Crystals, Cleanses, and Bubble Baths Not Included)*

"Shannon Watts shares a fresh and accessible model that anyone can follow to ignite their everyday life with more aliveness and meaning."

—**TARA MOHR**, author of *Playing Big: Practical Wisdom for Women Who Want to Speak Up, Create, and Lead*

"*Fired Up* offers a powerful process to honor the spark within."

—**SHARON SALZBERG**, author of *Lovingkindness: The Revolutionary Art of Happiness* and *Real Life: The Journey from Isolation to Openness and Freedom*

"Shannon Watts shows us how to turn small sparks into big, courageous actions at any age."

—**RESHMA SAUJANI**, author, activist, founder of Girls Who Code and Moms First, and host of the podcast *My So-Called Midlife*

Fired Up

ALSO BY SHANNON WATTS

Fight Like a Mother

Fired
Up

How to Turn Your Spark

into a Flame and

Come Alive at Any Age

SHANNON WATTS

THE OPEN FIELD • PENGUIN LIFE

VIKING
An imprint of Penguin Random House LLC
1745 Broadway, New York, NY 10019
penguinrandomhouse.com

The Open Field/A Penguin Life Book

THE OPEN FIELD is a registered trademark of MOS Enterprises, Inc.

Book design by Daniel Lagin

The epigraph on page xiii is from Audre Lorde, *I Am Your Sister:
Collected and Unpublished Writings*, Oxford University Press, 2009.

LIBRARY OF CONGRESS CATALOGING-IN-PUBLICATION DATA
Names: Watts, Shannon, author.
Title: Fired up : how to turn your spark into a flame
and come alive at any age / Shannon Watts.
Description: [New York] : The Open Field/Penguin Life, [2025] |
Summary: "From the founder of Moms Demand Action, a guide to harnessing
your potential, living without fear, and coming alive at any age" —Provided by publisher.
Identifiers: LCCN 2024044699 (print) | LCCN 2024044700 (ebook) |
ISBN 9780593831939 (hardcover) | ISBN 9780593831946 (ebook)
Subjects: LCSH: Self-actualization (Psychology) in women. |
Self-realization in women. | Aging.
Classification: LCC BF637.S4 W3946 2025 (print) |
LCC BF637.S4 (ebook) | DDC 155.2—dc23/eng/20250208
LC record available at https://lccn.loc.gov/2024044699
LC ebook record available at https://lccn.loc.gov/2024044700

Printed in the United States of America
1st Printing

The authorized representative in the EU for product safety and compliance is
Penguin Random House Ireland, Morrison Chambers, 32 Nassau Street,
Dublin D02 YH68, Ireland, https://eu-contact.penguin.ie.

MARIA SHRIVER
PRESENTS
THE OPEN FIELD
A PUBLISHING IMPRINT

BOOKS THAT RISE ABOVE THE NOISE AND MOVE HUMANITY FORWARD

Dear Reader,

Years ago, these words attributed to Rumi found a place in my heart:

> *Out beyond ideas of*
> *wrongdoing and rightdoing,*
> *there is a field. I'll meet you there.*

Ever since, I've cultivated an image of what I call "the Open Field"—a place out beyond fear and shame, beyond judgment, loneliness, and expectation. A place that hosts the reunion of all creation. It's the hope of my soul to find my way there—and whenever I hear an insight or a practice that helps me on the path, I love nothing more than to share it with others.

That's why I've created The Open Field. My hope is to publish books that honor the most unifying truth in human life: We are all seeking the same things. We're all seeking dignity. We're all seeking joy. We're all seeking love and acceptance, seeking to be seen, to be safe. And there is no competition for these things we seek—because they are not material goods; they are spiritual gifts!

We can all give each other these gifts if we share what we know—what has lifted us up and moved us forward. That is our duty to one another—to help each other toward acceptance, toward peace, toward happiness—and my promise to you is that the books published under this imprint will be maps to the Open Field, written by guides who know the path and want to share it.

Each title will offer insights, inspiration, and guidance for moving beyond the fears, the judgments, and the masks we all wear. And when we take off the masks, guess what? We will see that we are the opposite of what we thought—we are each other.

We are all on our way to the Open Field. We are all helping one another along the path. I'll meet you there.

Love, Maria S

To every woman who encouraged me
to turn my spark into a flame

You cannot, you cannot use someone else's fire. You can only use your own. And in order to do that, you must first be willing to believe that you have it.

—AUDRE LORDE

Contents

Author's Note

Throughout this book, I've attempted to acknowledge the many cultural and societal ways women are silenced or taught to silence themselves. That said, I certainly can't and don't claim or attempt to speak for *all* women. As someone who is white, cisgender, nondisabled, and heterosexual, I was born with a variety of privileges that many others don't have, which is why this book features the stories of so many other women with varying viewpoints and experiences. In writing about my own firestarter journey and the firestarter journeys of other women, I have strived to be as inclusive as possible. When I write the words "women" and "woman," I'm referring to anyone who identifies as a woman or who has felt the effects of living in a gendered world. If that includes you, I hope you see yourself reflected in these pages.

PART
ONE

How to
Start a Fire

stripped off my work clothes and held up the polyester hospital gown a doctor's assistant gave me to put on. It was definitely giving more "children's extra-large T-shirt" than "gown." All my clothes were already embarrassingly too tight after giving birth to my third child, and now this dress, seemingly made of one-ply toilet paper, was going to unlock a whole new level of humiliation. I put it on and turned my naked back to the wall, hoping the doctor wouldn't notice I was still wearing maternity underwear.

After hurriedly leaving work during my lunch hour for what I thought would be a quick appointment, I was told the doctor was running at least half an hour behind schedule. Years before the invention of smartphones, thirty minutes felt like an interminable amount of time to be alone with my many thoughts in a very small, very quiet exam room. To prevent myself from panicking about all the work piling up back at the office, I studied posters on the walls describing common conditions someone visiting a skin doctor

3

might suffer from . . . psoriasis, rosacea, hives. Almost all of them listed stress as a contributing factor.

Finally, a gentle knock on the door. "Hi there, I'm Dr. Miller. Sorry to be meeting you under these circumstances," said the middle-aged man in wire-rimmed glasses, walking directly over to the sink to wash his hands. Dr. Miller's office had had mercy on me, squeezing me onto his calendar for a last-minute emergency visit.

My eczema, which I'd attempted to keep at bay for years, was currently launching a full-scale attack on my body. After turning thirty, I'd noticed the itchy bumps popping up behind my knees and in the crooks of my elbows. My doctor at the time said the breakouts would go away if I "decompressed," a word that made me LOL before people LOLed. I had just had two babies twelve months apart, and I was due back at work in just six weeks—all the maternity leave I could afford, given the cost of daycare. I wouldn't be "decompressing" anytime soon. I left that doctor's office with only a referral for a therapist, which felt less like a remedy and more like one more thing I didn't have the time or the money for.

Instead of going to a therapist, I'd spent the intervening years trying to cure myself with an assortment of over-the-counter, off-label remedies—hypoallergenic lotions, vitamins, and supplements, even bathing in bleach—but the eczema continued its march across my body. First, it spread under my breasts and into my armpits. Then, it crept across my stomach and onto my thighs. Eventually, it engulfed my entire body in angry red patches that traveled up my chest and across my neck, scalp, lips, eyelids, and earlobes. What was once insidiously itchy now felt like fire, and it distracted me during the day and kept me awake at night.

Dr. Miller leaned in to examine my oozing skin and jotted some notes on an electronic pad. Then he sat back on his stool and looked at me earnestly.

"How much stress are you under?" he asked.

"How much time do you have?" I lobbed back.

Dr. Miller didn't laugh. We stared at each other for several seconds, and then I cracked. What started as a few quiet tears falling down my face turned into a torrent of sobs that soaked my child-size gown and the exam table paper I sat on. I leaned forward and put my head in my hands. Dr. Miller tenderly handed me a box of tissues and allowed me to weep on his exam room table, all the while patting my back and reassuring me, "It's okay, Shannon. You'll be okay."

For the first time in years, my guard was down. I'd spent my entire adult life trying to convince myself and everyone else that I was strong and impenetrable, but Dr. Miller's kindness and concern were like kryptonite. And now, in that vulnerable state, I was able to see clearly what my body had been trying to tell me for years, and it was so much bigger than just being overwhelmed. I'd made some very significant, very wrong choices, and if I wanted to get better, I would have to fix those mistakes. My eczema wasn't the sickness; it was a symptom of a life that was making me sick. There was no way to avoid it anymore: The only way to heal myself was to face both my fears and my fuckups. I was at a crossroads in my life, and no matter which direction I chose, there would be serious consequences.

After several starts and stops, I pulled myself together, got dressed, and left Dr. Miller's office—again with a referral for a therapist, but also a prescription for cortisone.

That evening, I didn't tell my husband about the meltdown I'd had in Dr. Miller's office. What was I supposed to say? "Hey, I had the epiphany today that my body is rebelling against the life we built together . . ." I couldn't tell him that the pressure of all the roles I'd taken on had become too much to shoulder. That each day at work, I felt I had to prove my value and protect my job by taking on more projects and staying later in the office than my single, childless, mostly male peers. And that each night when I got home, I had to do the same with caretaking and housework. That I resented sacrificing my own wants and needs to take on the responsibilities of supporting a family of five. That I regretted getting married so young.

It was that last thought that sent cortisol coursing through my body and sent my eczema into overdrive. Jayson and I had married a few months after graduating from college when we were just twenty-three. At the time, my parents were in the middle of a brutal divorce. After twenty-six years of marriage, my mother fell in love with a family friend, and soon after, my father started dating his secretary. It was beyond cliché, but it was also crushing. An only child, I knew instinctively that the end of their marriage was the beginning of the end of our nuclear family.

Desperate for some semblance of stability, I'd convinced Jayson to get married. A few weeks later, we exchanged vows over wedding rings we had bought at JCPenney. Three months later, I was pregnant. Three months after that baby was born, I was pregnant again. And by the time I turned thirty, I was a mother of three.

Because of the financial pressure to support our family, I deferred my dream of becoming an investigative journalist and took a job in public relations. It was the first job I was offered after graduation. Instead of writing articles about world events, I was writing press releases about products. And because I was such a young mom, I had little in common with other women my age, who were out having fun while I was at home changing diapers. I couldn't even afford an occasional date night out with my husband, who felt more like a roommate than a romantic partner.

And yet, to anyone looking in at my life from the outside, it might have seemed like I was living life in the fast lane. I was married to a perfectly nice person, we had three cute kids, we'd managed to put a down payment on a home, and I was climbing the ladder at work. I should have felt grateful, satisfied, even happy. Instead, I felt like I was on a highway going 100 miles an hour with no exits in sight, and only my body had realized the speed was unsustainable.

Instead of confiding in my husband, I went to my bedside table and took out a blank journal a friend had given me for my birthday. My initials were stenciled in gold leaf on its navy blue leather cover. At first, I'd thought about throwing it away. To me, a weary working mom of three, journaling seemed like the ultimate indulgence—a diversion for angsty women with too much time on their hands. At the last minute, I'd stashed the journal in a drawer. Now the journal's empty pages were inviting me to investigate what had happened in Dr. Miller's office. If I couldn't confess my fears to my husband, I would write them all down and see if they still made sense outside the confines of my brain.

Starting that night, I wrote in my journal every day for at least ten minutes. Some days, I dreaded having to put words on the page. Other days, my writing flowed so freely I struggled to close the cover. Eventually, an abstract of my life began to take shape, and I was able to see clearly all the ways—big and small—that I'd betrayed myself and ended up in a life I didn't recognize.

From a bird's-eye view, my journal told the story of someone who had transformed from a young girl with big dreams into an overwhelmed woman with crushing responsibilities. The more I wrote about what I wanted my life to look like, the closer I got to a truth so unsettling that it made me regret not throwing the journal away in the first place. After nibbling around the edges of what felt unspeakable for so long, I finally wrote, "I don't think I love my husband."

The words felt like both an unburdening and a catastrophe. I knew my admission would come at a steep cost—not just to me, but to my children. I also knew the only way out was through. So I began itemizing, like my daily list of to-dos, all the things I felt I deserved in love and in life. And when that list was complete, I wrote down all the things I thought were wrong with my marriage, including my own inadequacies and insecurities. I was self-aware enough to know that I was as culpable for my misery as anyone else. The lists took weeks to complete, but by the time I was done, the discrepancies were undeniable, resulting in both clarity and panic. If things were this off track, this early, what hope was there for our future? And then an even more daunting thought: What if things stayed this way forever? If I already felt unrecognizable to myself, who would I be in five, ten, or even twenty years?

I wasn't yet ready to answer those questions, so I just kept writing. And each night, when I put my journal back in the drawer of my bedside table, I inched closer to uncovering all the feelings I hadn't been able to face before my appointment with Dr. Miller. For the first time, I was examining what I valued and wanted, and I was imagining what it would look like to live in a way that prioritized those desires. With every reflection I put on the page, I was teaching myself how to live on fire.

1

What It Means to Live on Fire

My story isn't an uncommon one. So many women, especially when they reach midlife, wake up one day and realize they're living lives they didn't want or don't recognize. If you're reading this book, I'm guessing that you, too, feel or have felt the same way. Maybe you're in a job that doesn't light you up. Or you're with a partner you're not connected to. Or you're navigating life alone, without a circle of supportive friends. Or maybe, like I was, you're living at the mercy of other people's wants and needs, with obligations so all-encompassing that you don't have time to think about— let alone go after—what you truly want. At first, each of the identities you took on or the obstacles you faced might have seemed temporary, but then, over time, they added up, and now, suddenly, you're feeling lost, unmotivated, unfulfilled ... or maybe just meh. Instead of feeling alive, you feel at best like you're on autopilot and at worst as if you're squandering your life.

Maybe you're ashamed to want more.

Maybe you're so consumed by the demands and needs of others that you've neglected your own desires.

Maybe you haven't accomplished the things that really matter to you yet.

Maybe you're looking back on your life and realizing you've just been going through the motions.

Maybe your life is technically fine, but you don't yet know what you want. Or maybe you know what you want, but you're afraid it's too small or too inconsequential to matter.

Maybe you've convinced yourself that you've neglected your desires for so long that now it's too late to want or expect more.

But none of these fears are true; you're not too much, and it's not too late. I know this firsthand—it took me over four decades to begin living in a way that was invigorating, fulfilling, and true to me. Like too many other women, I'd spent much of my life allowing my fears to limit my life and my desires. It wasn't that I wanted or needed more stuff; I wasn't looking for a bigger house or a luxury car or a designer wardrobe. I just wanted that feeling of aliveness that comes from living authentically and meaningfully.

People who have come alive are clear on who they are and what they want. They ask themselves if they're actually living or if they're settling for the status quo. They make choices that prioritize their passions and energize them. They recognize the value they bring to every situation. And they pay attention to the voice that tells them there's more to life than what they're tempted to settle for (or have been told to settle for).

The voice that told me I couldn't live authentically, let alone audaciously, threatened to become the narrative of my life. But after my own journey, which included founding and leading Moms Demand Action, where I helped thousands of women transform feelings of hopelessness or powerlessness into feeling fired up in every aspect of their lives, I came to realize that there's a formula that every woman can follow to come alive, or to live on fire, a radical and even political commitment to building a life from the inside out, not the outside in. Because when women figure out what makes them come alive, they not only improve their own lives but also are more likely to improve the lives of others.

Why fire? Throughout time, fire has symbolized the wisdom, knowledge, and energy that can transform your life through purification, rebirth, and renewal. The life cycle of fire, from the spark that starts it to the ashes it leaves behind, symbolizes for me the process women can follow to bring about transformation in their lives. Fire gives us sustenance and life, it can burn away what no longer serves us, and it throws off the light and warmth that can summon your people.

For our purposes, living on fire is a metaphor for the journey of personal transformation—not the kind of transformation that makes you more youthful or famous or wealthy, but an internal shift that will help you see two things more clearly: what's limiting you and what's calling you. Those things will differ from one woman to another. For some, it might mean being more open to new experiences and relationships. For others, it could mean bringing new energy or more intensity to the things they're already doing. For others still, it could mean deciding to pause, slow down, and consciously do less than they were doing before. Living on fire might lead you to do extraordinarily ambitious things, but it also may compel you to finally act on ordinary things that are meaningful to *you*. Both are daring, and both are signs of a life on fire.

What you burn for may be as simple—or as significant—as having a hard conversation, asking for a promotion, going on a retreat, going back to school, volunteering in your community, having a child or deciding not to, moving to another city, ending a relationship, starting a new career, or putting an idea out into the world. Whether it requires you to do more or less in your life will depend on your fire and your goals. But, inevitably, you will have to do life *differently*. You'll need to build a life on your own terms—a life in which you get to decide what you do, where you go, and who you'll become. You'll need to take risks and commit to continuing them throughout your life. You'll need to challenge lifelong beliefs and shed the expectations of others. You'll need to experience—even embrace—your fears.

And that all starts with examining the experiences and emotions that dimmed your spark in the first place. What caused you to stop nurturing the unique energy inside you—the individual life force that is always there, waiting to be ignited? Because the truth is, no matter how hard you've tried to ignore or bury your spark, its energy *will* find a way out—either through anger, anxiety, depression, apathy, or resentment. Mine burned me from the inside out, resulting in a skin condition so severe it put me in an emergency room. But that experience—the realization that I wanted and deserved more from my life—was a turning point that led me to the formula for living on fire, a formula that helped me find the courage to end my marriage, reimagine my life, and eventually start Moms Demand Action, the world's largest field experiment for helping other women come alive. And since then, I've helped countless women nurture and unleash their own sparks to start fires that transform their lives.

I call these women "firestarters"—women who make the choice to prioritize their desires over societal expectations. They own their own narratives and trust themselves above all else, letting their desires guide them in life. They're fiercely alive and unapologetically themselves, taking risks and embracing failure, and they're always open to finding their next fire and following it—no matter where it takes them. And often, the transformations in their lives started not with a blaze, but a simple spark of curiosity or inspiration—from a volunteer meeting to a blog post to jotting down an idea to even just picking up this book—that grew into a blazing fire.

THERE'S A FIRESTARTER INSIDE YOU

Even before I had the words to describe what living on fire meant, I knew a burning woman when I saw one. As a young girl growing up in Fairport, New York, my state representative, Louise Slaughter, was a stay-at-home mom who said she felt compelled to come out of the kitchen to protect a small forest of beech-maple trees near her home that developers were threatening to cut down.[1] Thanks to Louise's activism, the forest survived, and that win fueled her next fire: running for public office. Louise became one of just a handful of women lawmakers in New York, and she made her reputation— first as a state lawmaker and later in Congress—by advocating for women's issues like medical research, reproductive rights, and violence prevention.

I remember watching the local news with my parents and being in awe of this woman who fully owned her power in an era when women were either prevented from having it or weren't comfortable flexing it. When I was twelve years old, I met Louise in person; my sixth-grade class was invited to march alongside her in Fairport's local Fourth of July parade. Just before walking the parade route, Louise looked me in the eye, shook my hand, and asked me my name. And even though Louise loomed larger than life to me, she wasn't at all intimidating—just incredibly confident. That day, she was gracious to everyone she came in contact with, she patiently answered constituents' questions, and she brushed off the occasional jeers from her (mostly male) opponents in the crowd.

Inspired by Louise, I had big dreams of fighting for equality and justice as a journalist. But as I got older, the obligations and obstacles of being a woman got in the way of those dreams. And there were so few firestarters in my orbit that I eventually lost sight of what living on fire could look like, or whether it was something I was even capable of. Similarly, you might be reading this right now and thinking that sure, you've done some meaningful things in your life, but you don't consider yourself a firestarter. Maybe you struggle to see the firestarter in you. You might be thinking, "How can I be a firestarter when I don't yet know what I burn for?" But that is the beauty of being a firestarter. You don't earn the title after you've built your first successful fire. You earn it the moment you recognize that you want more out of your life. You become a firestarter the second you decide you are going to start living on fire. To inspire and support you in your journey, I've collected dozens of firestarter stories of women from all walks of life—activists, teachers, entrepreneurs, athletes, artists, nurses, mothers, wives, friends, leaders, and more—to help you better understand what fires you up.

Firestarters are women like Sarah Hartley, a mom who started a magazine as a hobby to highlight taboo women's issues and bring them out into the light. As Sarah interviewed women about their struggles with mental health, infertility, body image, racism, and discrimination, it encouraged Sarah to be vulnerable, too. After she decided to fold her magazine, Sarah took the skills she acquired and parlayed them into a new career as a confidence coach, working with women on boosting their feelings of self-worth. "Creating that magazine changed how I walked through the world," Sarah says.

Firestarters are women like Gisele Barreto Fetterman, who decided to become a firefighter at age forty—right in the middle of her husband's campaign for a US Senate seat. Even though lots of people—including her husband and children—told Gisele it wasn't the right time to become a firefighter or that it was too dangerous, she enrolled in her local fire academy anyway, where she was the oldest person in her class and one of only two women. Today, Gisele is a Rivers Edge Volunteer Fire Department member and has been on nearly one hundred calls to fight fires. "This was just for me; a dream I'd had since I was a child, and I decided it was time to make it come true," Gisele says. "What I realized is that when I follow my passions, I'm more fulfilled, and that makes me a better partner, parent, and person."

Firestarters are women like Zoe Winkler Reinis, whose volunteerism with immigrant families at the US-Mexico border turned into an organization to help refugees, migrants, and asylum seekers. By focusing on the safety of women and families who needed support, Zoe was able to overcome lifelong insecurities about her struggles with neurodiversity and learning disabilities. Instead of hanging in the background and observing her life from the sidelines, advocacy brought Zoe to life, and she realized it was the key to helping her unlock her truest self—something that had been in hiding until she was almost forty years old. "For the first time in my life, I feel fulfilled," Zoe says. "And even though what I'm doing right now could take me down a million different paths in the future, I'll take my new sense of self with me wherever I go."

Firestarters are women like Amber Goodwin, who gave up on becoming a lawyer after she was rejected by seventeen law schools but, after Donald Trump was elected, decided she needed to try again. At age thirty-eight, Amber was attending law school and working full time, and at age forty, she was elected the first Black woman president of Mitchell Hamline's Student Bar Association. Amber is now a practicing prosecutor in Texas, and she's working to get more people of color represented in law schools. "Getting through law school and starting a whole new career midlife made me realize there's nothing I can't do," Amber says.

Firestarters are women like Carol Fricke, a retired teacher who became a creative writer in her seventies. Through countless hours of research and practice, Carol transformed herself from a novice who was unsure how to create a plot or write dialogue into an expert who could confidently tell a compelling story. After Carol finished her book, she sent it out to publishers, but it was rejected more than two hundred times. Finally, at age seventy, Carol became a published author. "Promoting my book forced me out of my comfort zone and into the world, and I know how to advocate for myself now," Carol says.

In addition to these women's stories and the stories of so many other firestarters, each chapter of this book includes exercises to help you light the match and actions that will help you fan the flames of your fire, all of which were informed by my experiences and the experiences of other women, as well as the trainings I developed for

Moms Demand Action. Through the lives and examples of these firestarters, you'll gain valuable insights and strategies for your own journey. And you'll realize that everything you need to become a firestarter already exists within you. Their successes and challenges will act as a road map for igniting your own fire, while the "light the match" exercises and "fan the flames" actions in each chapter will help you reflect both on where you are and where you want to go.

I recommend buying a notebook—maybe, like me, there's a forgotten one waiting for you in your bedside table—and claiming it as your firestarter journal. Writing helps us organize our thoughts and look at the events of our lives objectively. When used alongside this book, journaling will help you transform from someone who looks at firestarters in awe to a firestarter in your own right.

Like these women, you *are* a firestarter and you deserve to live on fire. You are allowed to explore who you are and what you want. You are entitled to act on the desires, values, and passions that energize you. And when you're at the end of your life, you have an obligation to look back and know that you created and lived a meaningful life that was faithful to who you are. To know you truly burned. Because no one is on earth to simply exist. If you're living your life, day in and day out, feeling disappointed or uninspired or numb, you have a right—even a responsibility—to do something about it . . . *now*. And I'm here to show you how.

2

What Your Fire Is Not

Before we talk about what living on fire is, it's important to get clear on what it isn't. Too often, society tricks women into believing we're living on fire when, in fact, we're just living by the rules of a system that was specifically designed to keep our desires in check, which leads to anxiety, isolation, and exhaustion—the opposite of aliveness. In order to get off that hellish hamster wheel, you'll need to recognize, unlearn, and push back on what you've been taught and internalized about your role in a white patriarchal capitalist society. Let's start by identifying some of the pitfalls to watch out for.

PURPOSE

Elizabeth Gilbert, author of several bestsellers, including the memoir *Eat Pray Love*, summed up the trap of purpose perfectly in an interview with Kate Bowler: "We've all been fed [this formula] and we've been fed it our entire lives. . . . Each of you is born with a special gift. . . . It's your job in life—your purpose—to uncover what that thing is. And then once you find it, you must foster it, master it, and curate it until you are at the top of that thing that only you can do."[1]

It is, in fact, an incredible amount of pressure to live life in the present while simultaneously peeking around every corner to hopefully, possibly stumble upon your purpose. The stress of finding a purpose has become such a widespread phenomenon that researchers have a name for it: purpose anxiety. Purpose anxiety is the fear and frustration that shows up either when you're trying to discover your purpose or when you think you've figured out what your purpose is and you're striving to achieve it. Researchers say purpose anxiety can result in feeling like a failure, making negative comparisons about yourself to others, or feelings of emptiness or being ungrounded.

But purpose anxiety doesn't go away just because you think you've found your purpose; we've all had the experience of wanting something desperately only to find in a few years or months that that desire has dimmed. Nazanin Boniadi, the daughter of Iranian parents who fled their homeland for England when she was a baby, grew up feeling compelled to attend medical school and become a doctor. A career in medicine would ensure she had a good, stable income and future. Even though she felt drawn toward activism and acting, she spent much of her life trying to turn her parents' purpose for her into something that she wanted, too. "I knew in my heart that I wanted to help people, so I convinced myself that medicine was an acceptable option. And I knew it would make my parents proud," Nazanin says.

Nazanin moved from London to California to pursue medical school. Fueled by a strong sense of duty, determination, and hard work, she earned her bachelor's degree with honors in biological sciences. Despite this success, she realized medicine wasn't her calling. "During class I was always thinking, 'This seems so much easier for other people; why is it torture for me?'" Nazanin says. After graduation, she says she had an epiphany: The purpose she'd been assigned by her family was never going to materialize because it wasn't her purpose; it wasn't fueled by any passion. Nazanin decided to forgo medical school to pursue acting and, within a year, landed a role on a soap opera. That opportunity served as a springboard into bigger roles in movies and on television, which opened the door for her to follow another passion: activism. Nazanin used her celebrity to bring attention to the struggles of women in Iran who were fighting for their freedoms. Not only did she become a spokeswoman for Amnesty International, but she even put her acting career on hold to focus full time on her activism during the anti-government uprisings in her homeland.

In hindsight, Nazanin says she realizes that looking for a purpose can prevent you from seeing clearly what you really want: "I now know that when something doesn't come naturally to you, you can't—and shouldn't—force it."

You, too, may be living your life *for* a purpose instead of *on* purpose. You may be waiting to be told what you should want instead of paying attention to what you truly want for yourself. If you're trying to find your purpose, you're searching for that one thing that will make everything else in your life suddenly fall into place. You're looking at your life as though it has a destination. You're looking for something to fall into your lap that will make you feel whole. But when you live on fire, you see the meaning in everything you do. You connect the dots and identify patterns in your life. Instead of waiting to be told what to do, you're taking it upon yourself to uncover what makes you come alive. In other words, when you're living *for* a purpose, you're asking yourself, "Why am I on earth?" When you're living *on* purpose, you're asking yourself, "How do I make the most of my time on earth?"

Even when we think we're looking for our purpose, we could realize later we went too far down the wrong path. Nazanin later realized that orienting her life toward one grand, singular purpose—one that she didn't really have passion for in the first place—stopped her from seeing all the experiences and opportunities that presented themselves to her along the way. In her heart of hearts, Nazanin knew what would make her feel fulfilled, but by focusing so much on her purpose, she neglected her spark.

If most of your attention is focused on the future, you're searching for a purpose, not finding your fire. Your fire is not a purpose; it's being purposeful—it's paying attention and then acting with intention. In the end, your life will not be determined by some mysterious, magnificent purpose but by all the smaller, more mundane things you choose to pay attention to along the way. Your thoughts and awareness influence the experiences you have, and those experiences determine the life you live. Eventually, those experiences will come together to tell the story of your life.

Purpose warning signs:

- You inherited or acquired your purpose instead of discovering it.

- You're not exploring people or ideas outside one specific purpose.

- You're not enjoying the process and your intuition is telling you it's time to move on.

HAPPINESS

Another message society sends us is that everything we do in our lives should lead to happiness, an eternal state of positive vibes that will fill us with contentment and simultaneously stave off suffering. But the problem with pursuing happiness is that, like all emotions, happiness is vague and ephemeral. For some people, happiness might be the avoidance of pain and suffering. For others, happiness could mean they lived a fulfilling life. For others, it could mean they attained wealth or fame. That's because happiness, at its core, is simply a state of mind. Whether you're happy at any given moment depends on circumstances you're unable to control, including your own thoughts and feelings.

Unsurprisingly, a growing body of research shows that having happiness as your life goal could actually make you miserable. A need to be happy, or happier, results in unrealistic standards that can result in not only disappointment but also loneliness. That's because being singularly focused on attaining a permanent state of happiness can cause you to hyperfocus on all the ways you lack happiness, preventing you from appreciating the smaller, simpler things in life that bring you pleasure. Instead of chasing happiness, firestarters find their fire in more tangible, albeit temporary, emotional goals like contentment, presence, and joy.

That's what Zerlina Maxwell, a political analyst who writes and speaks about cultural issues, learned when she graduated from law school. After spending years studying and sacrificing to graduate from a top 25 university, she got her law degree while also working as a paralegal, but instead of finding happiness, she found long hours, uncompelling clients, a competitive work environment, and no happy lawyers. Zerlina quickly realized that not only did she not want to be another unhappy lawyer, but her focus on long-term happiness had cost her short-term joy. "After spending so much time going after something that was going to make me unhappy, I decided that going forward I would apply a new filter to everything I did: 'What is it that lights me up *while I'm doing it*?'"

Zerlina's Twitter feed was so viral and so widely read by American pundits and politicians that even then presidential candidate Barack Obama took notice of her way with words. His online admiration turned into a real-life job for Zerlina when she was hired as a field organizer for Obama's 2008 campaign. And then, in 2016, Hillary Clinton, secretary of state, hired Zerlina to lead her presidential campaign's progressive and digital media outreach. Zerlina was finally following what lit her up, and it led her not only to a new career in politics, but eventually to jobs as a television analyst, a radio host, and an author. She has also applied her filter to her personal life. "Politics lights me up, but so does K-pop and golf," she says. "I'm not looking for a job to make me happy anymore; what's lighting me up right now is indulging in joy wherever I can find it, and that includes caring for myself and learning new skills."

We're all guilty of thinking or believing, "I'll be happy when..."

But happiness is a temporary state, not a life goal. As Oprah Winfrey and Arthur C. Brooks wrote in their book *Build the Life You Want: The Art and Science of Getting Happier*, "Happiness is not a destination, it's a direction. . . . The fact that complete happiness in this life is impossible might seem like disappointing news, but it isn't. It's the best news ever, actually. It means we all can finally stop looking for the lost city that doesn't exist, once and for all. We can stop wondering what's wrong with us because we can't find or keep it."[2] Instead of thinking, "I'll be happy *when* . . . ," firestarters acknowledge and appreciate the temporary but more tangible moments in life that light them up, like feelings of awe or wonder, glimmers of joy, and the sparks thrown off by the fires they've started.

Happiness warning signs:

- You're deciding what to focus on based solely on the immediate validation of "fun" or "happiness."

- You are always saying "I'll be happy when . . ."

- You focus on the happiness that big milestones or material items will bring instead of finding the potential for happiness in everyday moments.

ACHIEVEMENT

It's also easy to mistake your fire for achievement, especially in the Western world. If there's one thing Westerners love, it's success. If we don't stand to make money, build status, or receive praise as part of the process, we decide it isn't worth doing. For example, if you decide to take up a hobby—let's say baking—and you get good at it, others will ask you, or you might ask yourself, what comes next. One day, you're making muffins, and the next, you're Googling "How do I open a bakery?" You quickly forget that you started baking because you wanted to learn the craft of making a muffin, not to make money. It's fine to monetize your passion, but be wary of buying into the capitalistic mindset that tells you if something you love isn't generating income, it isn't valuable. Remember, your fire is for you; it doesn't need to earn its keep. If something speaks to the spark inside you, that is, in itself, enough reason to keep going.

Susan Piver tried to turn her passion into a business, and it went horribly wrong. It all started when the man she was in love with asked her to marry him. Susan was in her thirties, had never been married, and wondered whether she was marriage material. She decided to spend a whole month alone to figure out what she wanted, or, as Susan puts it, "to contemplate how someone could get married without bullshit, but with depth." She started writing down questions like "What will our home look like?" "What are our professional goals?" "Will we try to have children, and if so, when?" The answers Susan came up with made her realize she did want to get married, and she began to wonder if other couples might benefit from answering her questions, too. Susan ended up publishing a book called *The Hard Questions: 100 Essential Questions to Ask Before You Say "I Do"*. When it came out, it was a huge bestseller and turned Susan into a sought-after relationship guru overnight. Suddenly, Susan was being offered millions of dollars to write more books about self-help. She inked a new deal, but by the end of the negotiations, the new book she'd agreed to write wasn't at all what she wanted to write. "Unsurprisingly, it ended up being an awful book, it tanked, and everybody felt I had failed," Susan says.

After Susan and her publisher parted ways, she left the book publishing industry. She realized that to survive in that world, her values and desires would have to come second, if at all. Susan missed out on a huge payday, but she says the lesson she learned about not conflating the outcome of what you do with the process was priceless. "Don't base your interior design on who's going to live there. Don't paint a painting so that it sells in a gallery. And never write a book based on who will read it. Just start doing what you're passionate about, no matter how small, and do it for yourself," Susan says.

This advice is valuable even if you do end up commodifying your passion. Striving for achievements is not the same thing as finding your fire; it should feel like you're on an expedition to understand who you truly are, not on the hunt for money or status or clout. If you're always pushing yourself to hit that next milestone in your career or in your personal life, you probably aren't giving yourself enough time to rest and recharge, and that will lead to burnout. The pursuit of achievement tricks us into believing we need to earn our time on earth, but firestarters know the opposite is true. As long as you're staying true to your fire, you can be sure you're on the right path.

Achievement warning signs:

- You measure your worth by the results of your efforts and can't imagine a future beyond your current goals and plans.

- You constantly compare yourself to others.

- You lose sight of the side effects that come from experimenting, including joy and learning.

Yes, your fire may bring you a sense of purpose, happiness, or achievement, but it's important to remember that those are all benefits or by-products of the process, not the point of the process itself. If you're serving the system, you're focused on the outcome. If you're growing your fire, you're focused on learning to enjoy, or at least appreciate, the journey of growing your fire. Part of that journey includes collecting and assessing valuable information along the way: Can you do the work your fire requires? Does it light you up? Is it satisfying? Do you want to stick with it? Can you overcome any drawbacks you've discovered? Looking at your firestarting journey as a learning experience will help you detach from your preconceived notions about what you should do and move toward what you want to do.

3

Why Women Don't Live on Fire
and Why You Must Anyway

F alse fires" like purpose, achievement, happiness, and all the
other negative ideals society encourages us to chase are why so
many women's lives are long on responsibility and short on realized
desires. The good news is that there's a formula for living on fire; the
bad news is that following it will never be easy in a society that purposely puts up immovable obstacles to block you at every turn.
That's because society knows exactly what would happen if women
were allowed or encouraged to want: The world would come un-
done. Without the mental and physical energy of women propping
up the system, governments would fall, institutions would crumble,
and traditional family systems would fall apart. To ensure that
doesn't happen, society shoulders women with so many burdens
and responsibilities—from work to housework to caregiving—that
they have little to no room in their lives to explore their desires.

The true insidiousness of systemic inequality is what it convinces women to believe—or not believe—about ourselves, and for

many of us, the reclamation of our power has to begin in our own minds. We've been told we *should* live our lives in certain ways, and we learn to fear the backlash from the system if we dare to do otherwise. Women are told we *should* conform, we *should* be selfless, we *should* stay small (literally and figuratively), we *should* be good, we *should* be nice, we *should* be grateful. We *should* be content fulfilling our obligations while the men in our lives chase down their desires. Like so many women, I bought into these shoulds, too—I believed I should stay married, climb the corporate ladder, own the housework and childcare, always be busy and productive, stay a size four, and smile all the while.

These insidious shoulds take root in our minds, becoming so intractable that we begin to believe they're immovable facts of life. As a result, women's desires are hijacked by their obligations. Look around, and you'll see that men are encouraged to find fulfillment while women are trained to fulfill their obligations. And the more society tells women that they don't deserve what they want, the more we start to believe it. Eve Rodsky, a former lawyer who now studies America's problem with the gendered division of labor, refers to this phenomenon as "CIYOO," or "complicit in your own oppression." In Eve's studies of all the invisible tasks and mental load that fall on women's plates personally and professionally, she's found that capitalist patriarchy has really done a number on our psyches. "We start believing all the cultural messages we've absorbed," Eve says. "We think we should take pride in picking the florist for our wedding or sending that birthday gift to the in-laws or for wiping asses and doing all the dishes."

But Eve's studies also show that women can unlearn all the societal messages that contribute to their complicity, including challenging all the shoulds they've internalized by working on their liberation from the inside out. "When women realize how complicit they've been in their own oppression, they understand that it is a both/and requiring systemic change and individual agency to retire the toxic messaging. They're doing important work on themselves," she says.

Your fire starts where all your shoulds end. And in order to become a firestarter, you'll have to identify and extinguish all the shoulds you've internalized, along with all the negative beliefs that accompany them. Of course, it would be naïve to believe women can bypass or be unaffected by all the problems that plague society—certainly, they won't be fixed by any one individual overnight; it will take coalitions working together for decades or even generations to dismantle the systems in which constraints on women are a feature, not a bug. And while no book can help you completely avoid the realities of a rigged system, it is possible, and crucially important, that we learn from the women—especially BIPOC, queer, and disabled women who have had to balance an additional "shadow job," the burden of navigating a system rooted in racism, ableism, bigotry, and misogyny—who have figured out how to live *outside* the system. Women who don't just want to survive, but thrive. Women who crave aliveness. Women who know that when the system is rigged, the best way forward is to stop playing by its rules. And the stories of those women—women who have found new ways to change or upend the rules—will help you find the places in your life where you can identify, nurture, and, eventually, find your fire. As Amanda Doyle, cohost of the podcast *We Can Do Hard Things*, told me, "We need more stories of women trying hard to get things done and doing it, but in a new way—not trying to be a knockoff of the patriarchal version of a striver, because we've been told for so long that that's how we're supposed to do it."

While leading Moms Demand Action, I heard women voice the same doubts and excuses as to why they could not start living on fire. These bad beliefs feel deeply personal to each of us, but in reality, they're the products of a society that has trained women to devalue their wants and dreams. Unlearning these bad beliefs will be a messy, challenging process; every single firestarter I know has struggled, and often still does, to override the shoulds and obligations that hold them back from finding their fire. It's a process that will take time and patience and commitment, and it starts with naming all the reasons you have stayed on the sidelines. To help you begin, I've gathered some of the negative self-beliefs most commonly held by women and broken down why they're not accurate reflections of who you are but, instead, reflections of the messages society tells women about how they need to be. Read through the beliefs I've collected and explore which ones resonate with you the most. Have your journal ready to complete the "light the match" exercises and "fan the flames" actions that will help you dismantle these bad beliefs.

I'M NOT WORTHY

Let's start with the belief that you don't know what you want. Or maybe you do know what you want, but you don't believe you're worthy of investing the time, money, or space to cultivate it. After all, the patriarchy tells women that only exceptional women—the ones who have the determination to demand it—get what they want. As a result, you start to believe that if you haven't yet realized your passion or talent, you must not have or deserve one—that you're unworthy. This is a phenomenon Dr. Amy Diehl, a workplace gender bias expert, refers to as "self-limited aspirations." It's what happens when women decide it's not worth the drain on their energy, time, or mental health to take that next step forward. In other words, they decide it's easier to acquiesce than to fight against a system that was set up to make sure they fail. "Women look around and see all the difficulties other women around them are having, and then they make the very rational choice to give up," Amy explains.

Kelly Peters, a mom of two young boys in her forties, says her own self-limitations have held her back her whole life, and it started when she gave up on her dream of becoming an actor. Growing up, Kelly wrote plays and acted them out for friends and family. In high school, she excelled in drama club. Her teachers told her she was gifted and encouraged Kelly to go to college in Los Angeles to study acting. But instead of being inspired by other students, Kelly's inner voice told her she wasn't as good as they were and that she wasn't exceptional enough to succeed in Hollywood. "As soon as I started to doubt my worthiness and ability, I lost my desire," Kelly says. "I managed to convince myself an acting career wasn't worth the effort. After all, there are twenty thousand other people in Los Angeles who dream of becoming actors—why would I deserve it more than they did?"

Kelly ended up dropping out of college to take on odd jobs like nannying or working as a receptionist for a temp agency—work that didn't fulfill her creatively. But years later, after Kelly married and had kids, her passion for fashion reignited her creative desires. She started studying styling and carved time out to assist on magazine shoots and at fashion shows. Because she was so talented, Kelly was in popular demand, and she was forced to choose between her job as an executive assistant or becoming a full-time stylist. As much as she desired a career in fashion, once again, Kelly couldn't make the leap. "I always get so close, but then I tell myself that other women are more talented than me, that I need more experience, or that because I'm in my forties and haven't yet done the thing I want to do, I'll never be able to do it," Kelly says.

If, like Kelly, you're unsure how to tap into what you want, remember that, like everything in this book, learning what you want and how to go after it is a lifelong process, but knowing what you burn for is crucial to learning how to live on fire.

LIGHT THE MATCH

Reconnect with yourself

Write down twenty things you would do if money and time were no object. They can be big, like writing a novel, or small, like taking lessons to learn a new language. Then write down what's preventing you from doing those things right now. Now take that list and, for each category, set specific goals or intentions, including who could help you and the first action steps to start incorporating more of these desires into your current life.

I'M TOO BUSY

America's hustle culture has turned busyness into a status symbol. Women are told the more we do, the more we matter. Busyness is both a way of life and a badge of honor. If you're not working, you're driving your kids to extracurricular activities. If you're not volunteering, you're planning a friend's birthday. If you're not running errands, you're making a list of what needs to be accomplished before the end of the week. According to an analysis by Harvard Business School, the percentage of Americans who report they "never had enough time" rose 10 percent in the last decade. And a Pew Research survey found that six in ten adults in the United States say they're too busy to enjoy life.[1] I myself was guilty of this bad belief. In my job, in my volunteerism, and in my personal life, I always believed—at least subconsciously—that the more I took on, the more indispensable and important I became to the people depending on me to deliver. And the busier I became, the less I had to think about all the ways I wasn't actually fulfilled.

These psychological benefits of busyness distract us from feeling our deeper emotions; busyness makes us feel indispensable, as if we're the only person who can handle what needs to be done, and it can make us feel important when we're praised for taking on more. That's why it's easy for an outsider to mistake busyness for fire. But busyness actually prevents us from living fully by stealing the opportunities for relaxation, stillness, and self-reflection that are necessary to nurture your fire. Stephannie Lane Baker, deputy affiliate director with Emerge America, an organization that trains women to run for office, relied on busyness to help keep her anxiety at bay. Growing up, Stephannie immersed herself in academia and extracurriculars—including cheerleading, debate, yearbook, and choir—to avoid the anxiety that was exacerbated by a chaotic childhood. And when she became a parent, she leaned into the trope of the selfless mother to stay busy, which distracted her not just from her anxiety, but from a marriage that wasn't working. "I convinced myself that my value was based in how much I sacrificed and diminished myself for my children," Stephannie says.

During the pandemic, Stephannie finally began to see the extent of her addiction to busyness when she noticed her kids didn't miss having their afternoons filled with extracurricular activities. Stephannie was shocked that her kids were fine just to chill out at home with her. "I tried motivating them to be busier by telling them about all the things I used to do in high school," Stephannie says. "One day in the middle of my dialogue, my daughter interrupted me and said, 'Mom, I value my downtime more than that.' It made me realize that if rest and restoration were something my kids value, it was okay for me to value it, too."

Once Stephannie started to follow the example her kids set by valuing their own rest, she gave herself more grace to be less busy, too, and found herself using the extra time in her life to explore her own wants and needs. In addition to switching careers and volunteering, Stephannie began to confront the uncomfortable feelings she'd been avoiding with busyness. She turned inward and started to put a higher value on her self-care and rest while also making an effort to spend more time with the friends who filled her up. Stephannie realized her energy, effort, and focus were not unlimited resources. If you find yourself falling back on the belief that you're too busy to nurture your fire, remember that you deserve to value your time the way you value the time of others, and in order to nurture your fire, you'll have to invest in it.

FAN THE FLAMES

Conduct a time audit

Look at your schedule for the week. Is there something you can eliminate and replace with designated time to focus on your fire? Can you ask a neighbor to pick the kids up from school? Can you talk to your boss about making that pointless meeting a weekly email? It can be as little as twenty extra minutes, as long as those twenty minutes are completely yours to use as you wish. Now add that time to your calendar and mark it as "sacred."

I'M NOT QUALIFIED

So many of the women I've worked with and spoken to cite "imposter syndrome" as one of the main reasons they hold themselves back from going after what they want in life. Imposter syndrome is the belief—or the fear—that you're not enough. That you've somehow fooled everyone around you into believing you're better than you really are. That you don't deserve a turn even when the evidence shows you're just as deserving of praise or opportunities as anyone else. But no matter what you've achieved, there's a voice in your head that tells you to doubt yourself or to downplay your value.

The patriarchy purposely makes women feel they are never

fully ready to do the things they want to do while simultaneously encouraging men to go after whatever they want, even (especially?) when they're not qualified. Sure, we all worry we're out over our skis at some point, but experts say imposter syndrome is something women struggle with more than men. In one poll, over half of all women surveyed said they'd experienced imposter syndrome at some point in their lives, and two thirds of the women surveyed said they rarely feel confident due to feelings of self-doubt, incompetence, and being underqualified, particularly in the workplace.[2] Comparatively, over 50 percent of the men surveyed said they had never experienced imposter syndrome at all. And a study of high-performing executive women in the workplace found that nearly 75 percent of them experience imposter syndrome regularly. Even famous women—Viola Davis, former First Lady Michelle Obama, and Supreme Court Justice Sonia Sotomayor—have admitted to having imposter syndrome at some point in their lives.

Imposter syndrome is another type of "shadow job"—a constant mental drain that diminishes your confidence and makes it less likely you'll seek out or take on new opportunities. It can hold you back from making new friends or seeking out romantic relationships and even make you self-conscious about your parenting choices. But it's important to remember that the voice that convinces you you're just moments away from being exposed as a fraud isn't a reliable narrator.

It took a long time for Dr. Annie Andrews, a South Carolina pediatrician who attended college and medical school for eight years and then practiced as a pediatrician for fifteen years, to learn that lesson. She admits that she still feels like an imposter in certain spaces. "I always fear I'm not up to the task or I'm not good enough or I'm faking it," says Annie, who also ran for a seat in Congress. "I'll walk into rooms of wonderfully friendly lawmakers or surgeons or researchers and think, 'Oh well, I'm just a pediatrician and a mom,' despite the fact that my résumé would suggest that I have every right to be in those rooms."

Annie had always harbored the fear that someone at her hospital would realize she wasn't good enough to deserve a spot alongside her peers (most of whom were men). She found that the feeling followed her into other parts of her life, including advocacy. After a national shooting tragedy, Annie thought about joining Moms Demand Action but stayed on the sidelines, assuming her local chapter didn't want or need her. It wasn't until after the mass school shooting in Parkland, Florida, that Annie overcame her insecurities and became a volunteer, using her status as a physician to advocate for regulating guns to protect children. Years later, when Annie ran for a seat in Congress, she found her imposter syndrome rearing up again. "During my stump speeches, I'd say, 'This is what I've done, but there's nothing special about me—anyone could do what I've done,'" Annie says.

Annie's impulse to downplay her accomplishments is part of the reason it can be so difficult for women to celebrate their successes when they happen. That's because women are judged more harshly than men for self-promotion and, as a result, are more likely to downplay their accomplishments than promote them. Combine that with the good-girl conditioning that tells women to never do anything that could come across as boastful or arrogant, and many women decide it's easier to hide their light than to let it shine. It's no surprise, then, that most women I know would rather get a root canal than talk positively about themselves in public.

Now that Annie is older, she's better able to appreciate all the ways she's stepped up, something that has helped her to stop viewing herself as an imposter. "Perspective helped me stop giving a shit about all the insecurities that held me back," Annie says. "Now I can confidently say there is something special about me, and I've done a lot of things that other people haven't done."

The good news for those of us who struggle with imposter syndrome is that there are effective, easy ways to silence those negative voices in our heads telling us we aren't qualified enough. Try the "light the match" exercise below to help quiet that voice.

LIGHT THE MATCH

Create a fact sheet

Imposter syndrome can make you believe you haven't done enough or don't know enough, preventing you from seeing yourself clearly. Overcoming imposter syndrome can be a lifelong process, but one trick I've found helpful is to focus on the facts. To give you some real perspective, make a list of everything you've accomplished in your firestarter journal . . . and I mean everything. Start with the big accomplishments you remember each year going as far back as possible. Commit to adding to that list of milestones every week. Did you meet your deadlines at work? Did you plan a friend's surprise birthday party? Did someone ask you for advice? Then, any time you feel like a fraud, pull out your list for a reminder of all the things you've accomplished in your life. You'll be surprised by how much you've done and the expertise you've gained along the way.

I MIGHT FAIL

Too many women feel they're not allowed to make mistakes, that everything they do must be perfect, and if it's not perfect, they've somehow failed themselves and society. That's because the patriarchy tells us that worthy women are perfect women. If you fail, or you're bad, or you're messy, you're unworthy—of love, of desire, of being in the spotlight. This perfectionism is a no-win situation for women; when we place so much stock in the outcome of everything we do, we set ourselves up for disappointment, because no one is perfect.

My own perfectionism manifested in something I came to refer to as "post-appearance performance anxiety." As Moms Demand Action's spokesperson, I was regularly called on to appear on television—either to react to a shooting tragedy or to talk about policy, and even to debate detractors. The appearances themselves didn't scare me—I'm a good communicator; it was watching my appearances afterward that filled me with anxiety and dread. I would ruminate about everything from my physical appearance to the things I forgot to say or should have said differently, and no matter how many people told me I did a good job, I felt like a failure. Eventually, I started deferring invitations to go on television to other team members just to avoid the suffering I knew would come from judging myself afterward.

That's why perfectionism is so harmful: When you inevitably make a mistake, the self-criticism that follows can hold you back from wanting to try anything new. This is the vicious cycle that keeps women on the sidelines: Men fail and keep going; women fail, and they quit. If you want to nurture your fire, you'll have to get comfortable taking risks and making mistakes.

For some women, perfectionism is the persistent and harmful legacy of a difficult relationship. Stephanie Lundy, a former fashion and interior designer, grew up as an only child in a military family that frequently moved across the country. A sensitive and creative kid, Stephanie's demanding dad believed yelling at her and shaming her would toughen her up. If Stephanie was shy, her father called her Bambi; if she gained weight, he called her chubby. "Any mistake I made, no matter how small, was fatal in his eyes. And what he saw in me as flawed, I began to see as flawed, too," she says.

Stephanie's father's demand for perfection in everything she did ended up making her a perfectionist. To this day, she is terrified of getting any kind of criticism—even gentle feedback. If she makes a mistake—even a very small one—it can take her weeks to move on. And even though Stephanie has a degree in design and decades of experience in her field, that perfectionism has held her back in her career. "Any time I've made a mistake at work, I've convinced myself that the only honorable thing to do is to walk away from a job I loved," says Stephanie, who walked away from her career in fashion because she feared failure. "There's a list a mile long of things that I could have been successful at if it hadn't been for my fear of being judged by others and myself."

Stephanie is determined to overcome her perfectionism, and in addition to severing ties with her father, she's in therapy to find a way to reject the bad belief that if something isn't perfect, it isn't worth doing. "I've realized the best way to unlearn my fear of failure is allowing myself to fail and seeing that I can survive it," Stephanie says. "That feeling is better than living with the constant fear that someone will find fault with me. It's an unrealistic expectation and not one that I—or any woman—will ever be able to meet."

You, too, may have decided it's easier to stop trying new things or taking risks so you don't ever have to feel the shame of not meeting others'—or your own—high standards. But trying new things and inevitably failing at some is part of the process of learning to live on fire. The only way to overcome your fear is to prove to yourself that new experiences can't kill you. In fact, forcing yourself into new situations is a way to get you out of your comfort zone and give you that first boost of confidence you need to keep going.

LIGHT THE MATCH

Reframe your perceived flaws

If you know that you struggle with perfectionism, reflect on a recent moment when you felt those tendencies act up. What thoughts circulate when you feel the pressure to be perfect? In your firestarter journal, write down all those thoughts and then write a rebuttal to each one.

What pains me the most when I think about women who never learn or are never taught to live on fire is that they might spend their whole lives believing these false narratives about themselves. If I've learned one thing from spending so much time with Moms Demand Action volunteers, it's that our personal pain and struggles are made more bearable by sharing them with others. So much of the value of living on fire is coming together with like-minded women and realizing your challenges are not unique or insurmountable. Through that vulnerability, we're able to see that the negative ideas we hold about ourselves are not our own—they're simply societal messages we've absorbed and come to believe. When we recognize the truth, we can start to view the ideas we once held as facts about ourselves for what they truly are—fiction.

WHY YOU MUST LIVE ON FIRE

Women don't fear their fire because they're weak—it's because they're wise. They know there is a price to be paid for being a woman who wants, for being a woman who is always looking for new ways to feel fired up. Even as young girls, we see all the obstacles in our way—from gendered expectations to sexist stereotypes to patriarchal punishments—and we decide it's easier and safer to stick with the status quo. So we learn to keep our heads down and our desires in check. But together, throughout this book, we're going to unlearn that conditioning by imagining what life would be like if the only question you asked yourself was "What do I want?"

I didn't know what I wanted until I was in my forties when I started the largest women-led nonprofit in the nation. I was an introvert who struggled with severe ADHD and a debilitating fear of public speaking. I knew little to nothing about politics, organizing, or gun violence. Not exactly the description of someone people would point to and say, "She should take on the most powerful, wealthy special interest that's ever existed." And yet that's exactly what happened. Despite a myriad of imperfections and a lack of preparedness, I stepped up. In the face of obstacles that seemed insurmountable—some I'd constructed inside myself over a lifetime, others built by society—I persevered. In spite of my fear of public speaking and stepping into the spotlight, I summoned the courage to put myself out into the world. For over a decade, I led an army of angry Americans into battle against the gun industry, and together, we passed hundreds of gun safety laws; stopped the gun industry's agenda in statehouses 90 percent of the time; elected thousands of candidates who supported commonsense gun reform to office, including our own volunteers; and passed the first federal gun legislation in a generation. Turns out, this neurodiverse, reserved, middle-aged mom in the Midwest was exactly the right person for the job.

But early on, I was constantly told that what I was trying to do wasn't needed, or it couldn't be done, or I wasn't the right person to do it. When confronted with a choice to stay small and let the moment pass me by or step off the sidelines and into my power, finding my fire helped me meet the moment. In the years since, I've encouraged thousands of women to get off the sidelines of their lives by coaxing out their desires and stories, teaching them to stand up for themselves and others, and encouraging them to take on roles they never imagined they were qualified for. I've helped them find the fire inside themselves and then held their hands as they opened new doors and walked through them. That's what we are doing now. And then later, using what you learn, you'll do the same for other aspiring firestarters in your life.

LIGHT THE MATCH

List the firestarters you admire

In your firestarter journal, list three to five firestarters you admire in the public sphere (these can be celebrities or politicians) and three to five firestarters you admire in your community. Write down all the firestarting qualities you see in each of them that you'd like to cultivate in yourself. For the firestarters in your community, can you send them a short note or pull them aside the next time you see them and ask how they found their fire?

FAN THE FLAMES

Assemble your firestarter team

List three to five people you feel you can reach out to and share your fiery dreams with. Talk with them openly about your journey to begin starting fires in your life and be honest with them about why you see them as a source of support for that venture. Let them know you want to make them a part of your firestarter team, the group of people you intend to lean on as you embark on this journey toward a life on fire.

In a world that wants women to make themselves smaller and smaller until they disappear, making a conscious choice to live fully and authentically is a radical, even political, act. It takes incredible strength and courage to claim your right to exist fully, to be seen, and to be heard. By choosing to live on fire, you're not just allowing yourself to live the life you want and deserve; you're lighting the way for other women to do the same. Consider yourself a beacon—your fire will spark something in other women, proving to them that it's possible to break free from their constraints and live audaciously. This is the ethos of living on fire, and I know you're ready for what comes next. Time to get fired up.

PART TWO

Your Fire Formula

was fifteen minutes late for my yoga class. I hugged the wall as I entered the room and walked as quietly as possible to a spot on the outer edge of the class. Our teacher, who was standing at the front in a Christmas-themed yoga ensemble, asked if we had any questions about next week's final exam. After a lengthy question-and-answer session, she instructed us to move into a cat-cow pose. I stayed seated, gobsmacked. There was no mention of the mass school shooting. The rest of the class moved onto their hands and knees in unison. Was it possible I was the only person who was completely wrecked by what had just happened in a Connecticut classroom?

For months, I'd been preparing to get my yoga teaching certificate, a practice that helped me keep my stress (and eczema) in check. But at that moment, I couldn't fathom pretending to care about cat-cows. I was so full of rage that mindfulness wasn't even in the realm of possibility. I didn't want to stay centered; I wanted to channel my unadulterated anger into action. As my classmates exhaled long, loud pranayama breaths, I looked up at the clock—there were four more hours of class. I knew that if I left early, I wouldn't be allowed to take the test for my certificate the next week, but in the aftermath of the murders of twenty-six children and teachers, becoming a yoga instructor didn't matter anymore. During the next break, I grabbed my belongings and bolted.

At home, I walked directly into the kitchen, where my laptop was charging on the counter. I opened a Word document on my computer and listed all the ways I might be able to get involved in gun violence prevention. I could donate to an organization. I could meet with lawmakers. I could become a gun safety activist. That last one gave me pause. The word "activist" sounded subversive. After getting divorced, finding love again, and remarrying, I was a busy mom of five. I'd never been political. Becoming an activist felt foreign, if not fringe. But what if I joined a group of fellow angry moms? Surely a mainstream organization like Mothers Against Drunk Driving (MADD), which had changed the culture of drinking and driving in the 1980s, already existed for guns.

As a teen, I'd watched from my classroom window as MADD volunteers towed a car in front of my Texas high school. The car, crumpled from a collision and still splattered with victims' blood, sent a powerful message: This could be you. The other message it sent: These moms weren't fucking around. I wanted to stand shoulder to shoulder with a similar badass army of women who would refuse to allow any more children in our country to be killed by gun violence. As I imagined a tsunami of determined, angry women coming for the National Rifle Association, the ache of my despair was momentarily dulled by my desire to burn down the gun lobby.

I Googled "organization like MADD for gun control." No relevant matches came up. Google gave me only links to think tanks in Washington, DC, mostly run by men, and some one-off city and state organizations, also mostly run by men. After searching for almost an hour, I gave up. Where was the MADD for gun violence? I closed my web browser and clicked into Facebook. I only had seventy-five Facebook "friends," but almost all of them were mothers who were also reeling from the Sandy Hook School shooting. These were my people.

I created a new Facebook page called "One Million Moms for Gun Control" and wrote my first post: "I started this page because, as a mom, I could no longer sit on the sidelines. I'm too sad and too angry. Women were a hugely impactful force in the 2012 election, and we could do that again on this issue. Let's march in DC in 2013 and demand the reinstitution of the assault weapons ban, among other practical laws that would limit access to guns in America. Don't let anyone tell you we can't talk about this tragedy now—they said the same after Virginia Tech, Gabby Giffords, and Aurora. The time is now. Please share this link."

I was both energized and terrified by the idea of taking this bold step on my own. My career in communications had prepared me to promote products and people, but the brand I wanted to create was different—it was personal. I wanted to embolden women to stand up to the most powerful special interest that had ever existed. And if they responded to my clarion call the way I thought they might, my new life would be turned upside down. After my divorce, I'd remarried, and my new husband John and I were still in the thick of blending our family of five kids, a delicate ecosystem that required constant oversight. But the shooting ignited my most visceral instincts, and I knew there was no returning to the person I had been before it happened.

My soul had been insulted. I couldn't stand the thought of living in a world where children's safety was anything but the top priority. The only way to stay sane was to act.

My post disappeared into Facebook's ether. Would it connect with all the other women and mothers out there who were hurting as much as I was? I got up from the table to let the dogs out. A few minutes later, when I sat back down and refreshed my feed, the likes on my post were ticking up like seconds on a clock, and the comments were coming in so quickly that by the time I had read one, five new comments had been added. And all of them said: "How do I do this where I live?"

4

Finding Your Fire Formula

Even though journaling led me to the epiphany that I needed to make some major changes in my life, there was no clear path toward the aliveness I craved. I knew I wanted more freedom and time for desire, and I also knew I needed to have fewer roles, duties, and obligations. So over the next few years, I experimented and took risks, big and small. I got divorced. I left my job and started several new businesses (most of which failed). I became a practicing Buddhist. I started meditating and took up yoga. I took some graduate courses in creative writing. I sold my house. I said goodbye to friends who didn't fit into my life after my divorce. I went on a weekend retreat with strangers. I took my kids on road trips to new places. I now realize that all those actions—trying new things I knew might not work out and leaving behind people and places I thought would be part of my life forever—were a way of practicing intention; I was figuring out what I wanted, what I valued, and what I was good at.

Working through this process, which I now realize was my first earnest attempt to live on fire, was challenging. Some days, after an exciting meeting or a great afternoon spent with my kids, I was sure I had figured "it" out. Other days, I felt like nothing was ever going to satisfy me. I worried that I was chasing something that didn't exist and that all the people who warned me about wanting more for myself were right. But then there were the days in between, when I noticed small sparks, like a potential new friend or a skill I didn't realize I had, that energized me and helped refine the search for my first real fire. These were signals that I likely would have missed before. But once I put my wants and needs front and center in my life, I became far more attuned to my desires, my values, and the abilities I had to offer the world. Every day was filled with new discoveries about myself. It was exhilarating.

This process of self-discovery was what led me to start Moms Demand Action, where I figured out the formula for living on fire—a recipe for aliveness. I realized the journey I went through to find my fire was not unique. I watched the incredible women I worked with at Moms Demand Action, women who did not initially see themselves as leaders or activists, follow the same steps to aliveness that I did. They tried new things. They explored their interests. When things didn't go as planned, they saw an opportunity to learn, not a failure. Their transformations were powerful and inspiring. I found them even more remarkable because these women were not actively seeking a life on fire as I had, yet they had used similar steps to ignite their passions and their lives. This made me wonder: Could I use our collective experience to develop a formula to help guide other women who know they want to live on fire but aren't sure how? The answer was yes.

The formula I created starts with identifying the three elements of your fire triangle, mirroring the simple scientific model used to explain how fires work in real life. Each side of the fire triangle represents an element required to bring fire to life: heat, oxygen, and fuel. When these three elements are combined in just the right way, a fire can be ignited. But if any of those elements are missing or removed, a fire either won't start or will go out. Similarly, your fire triangle is made up of your unique heat (your desires), oxygen (your values), and fuel (your abilities). When all three of those elements are activated at the same time, your fire will ignite. This is the sweet spot where what you long for is aligned with what grounds and guides you, as well as your gifts, talents, and skills. It's an alchemy that can feel like magic, a profound or transcendent force that, for me at least, feels like touching the divine.

I wasn't able to start Moms Demand Action because I'm extraordinary; I was able to start it because I followed a specific formula. The women you see online or in person who are living lives you aspire to live aren't unicorns either; they're not any more talented or determined or passionate than you are. The only difference between you and those women is that they've figured out how to bring their desires, values, and abilities into alignment. Any woman can become a firestarter by following the formula and activating their fire triangle. And that starts with defining your own unique elements:

> **Desires.** Your desires are your deepest longings—the parts of you that yearn to be seen, to make an impact, and to be shared with the world. These are the longings that are now ready to be acted on. Because your desires are the **heat** that activates your fire triangle, it's the most powerful element among the three.

Values. Your values are your personal beliefs and principles that define your priorities, decisions, and actions—it's how you determine what is truly important to you in life. In your fire triangle, your values are the **oxygen** that feeds your desires.

Abilities. Your abilities are your unique mental or physical gifts, talents, and skills. They can be either innate or acquired, and they set you apart from everyone else. In your fire triangle, your abilities are the element that **fuels** your desires.

What's so profound about the fire formula is that it instantly turns anyone who wants to live on fire into a firestarter. When I started the process of trying to find the aliveness I so desperately wanted, I struggled to see myself as "successful." I felt that until I found my fire and the confidence I assumed would come with it, I was stuck with the label of "work in progress." I thought that my transformation only became meaningful when I arrived at its imagined destination. Not only was this thought pattern misguided, it robbed me of the pride and recognition I deserved to give myself for the act of simply trying. Sometimes I think about how my journey might have been different if I'd celebrated the strength and courage the process required from the start. If I'd seen every step forward and every risk taken as a victory, and treated myself with more kindness and compassion along the way. Maybe it would have been more fun. Maybe if I'd claimed my power sooner, I—and the world—would have seen me as a firestarter sooner, too.

The formula isn't about finding the perfect combination of desires, values, and abilities on your first try. In fact, if you are looking at the formula and thinking to yourself, "Sure, that sounds interesting, but I have no idea what my desires, values, or abilities are," that's okay. The only element you need to bring to the formula to make it work is your willingness to show up and commit to the journey of trying to live on fire every day. Once you make the decision to pursue a life of aliveness and fulfillment by utilizing the fire formula, you are living on fire. Full stop.

Throughout this process, you'll go through constant change. Your desires will shift. You might find that the values you thought you held are no longer important to you or the skills you thought you could rely on aren't going to take you far enough. More likely than not, you will start a fire only to discover that it doesn't burn as brightly as you hoped. That is okay. You are still a firestarter. Every attempt, even the ones that flicker and burn out, bring you closer to understanding what truly fires you up. As long as you return to your fire formula again and again, you are a firestarter.

This formula is your foundation for a life on fire. It puts the focus on the messy, uncertain, and often uncomfortable process that most people tend to gloss over when they talk about the story of their lives. Instead of constantly looking forward to a specific goal or milestone, you'll learn to see the challenges and the thrills of this process as the ultimate reward. Every mistake, every uncomfortable step outside your comfort zone, every doubt faced and overcome, is part of the fire you're building within yourself. Those acts of courage and resilience are what make you a firestarter, not the strength or size of the fires you cultivate.

In these next chapters, we'll unpack each side of the fire triangle and explore how it shows up in you and in your life. Using firestarters who have been through this process as examples, you'll learn how to identify your desires, values, and abilities and see how these elements are already present in your life. You'll learn the principles of each element, what they feel like, what they look like, how you can cultivate them, and how you can intentionally work to channel them toward your fire. You'll see through the stories of other firestarters that it can often take a few tries before finding the desires, values, and abilities that will ignite your greatest fires. And through the exercises that will help you light the match and the actions that will help you fan the flames, you'll learn how to embrace the ups and downs of this rewarding process. Being a firestarter means you value the journey as much as the outcome, because it is through the journey that you will truly come alive.

5

Finding the Heat
of Your Desires

The first thing that comes to mind for most people when they see the words "women" and "desire" in the same sentence is sexual lust or pleasure. For millennia, women's desires have been tightly knit to their sexuality; instead of women simply wanting, desire is shorthand for women who want to be wanted. As a result, women's desires have come to be seen as something that needs to be controlled and restricted rather than encouraged and nurtured. That's because when a woman knows what she wants and goes after it, she gets closer to knowing herself and asserting her power. As Audre Lorde said, "Our visions begin with our desires."[1] This is why the first step in activating your fire triangle is acknowledging what you desire, so you can begin to envision the types of fires you want to start in your life.

For the purposes of your fire triangle, your desires are not your sexuality but your source of heat—these are the burning desires that push you to act. As you become more in touch with the dreams you write about in your firestarter journal, you'll find that your desire to achieve them will become stronger and more present in your mind. This desire is the heat that rises inside you when you think about how you long to show up and be seen in your life or in the world, how you want to make an impact, how you want to grow and evolve. That heat is always present—whether you feel it right now or not—and it's pulling you toward an idea, experience, or outcome that, if you act on it, will bring you personal pleasure or peace. And even if it seems like your desires ebb and flow, rest assured that they haven't disappeared, no matter how long you may have denied them.

Every firestarter has her own heat story, a moment when her burning desires became so strong she had no choice but to act. Maybe the heat rising inside her was projected outward, leading her to speak up for herself or to take a stand, or maybe her heat stayed inside, but it helped her get still and listen to her intuition. When I first learned to live on fire, I was driven by the burning desire to live a life I wanted. But later, when I started Moms Demand Action, my burning desire drove me to protect the lives of others. As you begin building out your own fire triangle, you'll start by learning how to identify your desires and how to recognize your heat, lifelong practices that will help you live on fire.

During my interviews and work with firestarters over the years, I've noticed that women often describe similar sources of heat driving their desires, the most common being strength, faith, mission, intuition, and anger. Read through the stories of how heat manifests for these firestarters and think about which ones resonate with you. You may even start to recognize the moments of heat in your own life and use that knowledge to start your own fires.

STRENGTH

Strength is the bold power to face challenges head-on with courage, determination, and resilience. But it's also the quiet compassion, patience, and ability to trust your desire and lean into your vulnerability. Most of all, it's a profound, unstoppable belief in yourself. The energy your desire generates doesn't depend on the actions of anyone else or your circumstances. It comes solely from inside you; your inner strength becomes outer strength.

When Gretchen Carlson describes her strength, she refers to it as the fire in her belly that has helped her stand up for herself and others since she was little. It's no surprise, then, that in 2016, Gretchen found the fortitude to file a lawsuit against then Fox News chairman and CEO Roger Ailes—one of the most powerful men in media—alleging that he'd sexually harassed her in the workplace. Because of Gretchen's strength and public courage, dozens of other women stepped forward with their own accusations against Ailes, who was forced to resign. But Gretchen's journey didn't end there. As part of her settlement with Fox News, Gretchen had to sign a nondisclosure agreement that legally prevented her from sharing the details of her harassment, but she also demanded that Fox make a public apology. "I wanted an on-the-record apology because I knew I wouldn't be able to tell my side of the story, but the apology would prove to the world that I wasn't lying," she says.

It would have been easy for Gretchen to dismiss her desire for an apology as too much or unnecessary. Another person might have told herself she had already made her point and it was over-the-top to want more. But Gretchen stayed true to herself and demanded what she wanted. After her lawsuit was settled, Fox made an un-precedented public apology.

Signs your heat is strength:

- You have a history of standing up for yourself or others.

- You don't back down from what you know is right.

- People see you as a source of support.

FAITH

Sometimes heat can feel like faith—an inspirational, even tran-scendent, call-and-response with the universe that connects you to your desires. That heat might be spiritual or secular, but it's like finding a piece in the puzzle of your life that was missing. As part of Caitlin Crosby's faith, the question she most often asked during prayer was "How can I be of service?" She got an answer in her early twenties, after she started a small business selling necklaces and bracelets made from vintage keys. Caitlin paid a locksmith to en-grave the keys with inspirational words like "strength" and "fear-less" and encouraged people to embrace the word on their key and then pass it on to someone who might need it more. One day, when Caitlin was leaving church, she was walking down Hollywood Bou-levard and ran into an unhoused couple living in a cardboard box and holding up a sign that said "Ugly, broke, and hungry." Their sign, which reminded Caitlin of the words on her keys, made her stop and talk to the couple. That night, she took them to dinner, and the woman, who was wearing a beaded necklace, told Caitlin she was passionate about making jewelry. "That was my aha moment," Caitlin says. "I realized they were the missing link to my jewelry business, and I asked them on the spot to be my business partners."

Caitlin bought engraving equipment from a locksmith and hired the couple to engrave the Giving Keys at eight dollars per key. After she hired the couple, they were able to save enough money to rent an apartment. Fifteen years later, Caitlin's social enterprise has employed over 150 people transitioning out of homelessness and sold close to two million keys worldwide, including to celebrities like Taylor Swift, Kristen Bell, and Selena Gomez. Giving Keys has been a successful business, but, more important, it's been a successful tool for Caitlin to fulfill her desire to serve others. "My whole life I prayed every day, 'God, I want to feel what you feel for people. Give me your heart.' And I always say I feel like God answered that prayer with the Giving Keys."

Signs your heat is faith:

- You believe in a power higher than yourself.

- You are guided by prayer or meditation.

- You trust in your fire to unfold.

MISSION

Some people feel the heat when they decide to take on a task or a role that they consider to be their mission; a significant quest that becomes the "why" for everything they do. A mission can give you focus and direction, clarify your values, and make it easier to overcome whatever else in your life stands in the way of achieving your goal. Lucy McBath found her mission after her teen son, Jordan Davis, was shot to death at a Florida gas station. Jordan and his friends had stopped to buy some gum; Jordan was sitting in the back seat of a friend's car. A middle-aged white man pulled up in a car next to the boys and began arguing with them about the "loud music" they were playing. The argument escalated and the man pulled out a gun and fired ten shots into the car, hitting Jordan three times and killing him.

In the weeks after the shooting, Lucy felt compelled to tell her story to anyone who would listen. "I wanted people to see how devastated I was because I thought maybe that would be a way that people would begin to listen. It felt like no one was talking about how this was happening in communities all around the country, especially communities of color. I couldn't understand why people weren't up in arms over the large percentages of people dying."

Just a few months after Jordan's murder, Lucy, who had been a Delta flight attendant for thirty years, retired to become a full-time gun safety advocate and spokesperson for Moms Demand Action. "Slowly but surely, I began to recognize I wanted to be on the front line of activism more than I wanted to be on a plane," Lucy says. "I felt called to stand up for people who didn't have a voice and try to shine a light on gun extremism."

Later, Lucy ran for and won a seat in Congress. And in honor of Jordan, she unapologetically put ending gun violence at the top of her campaign priorities. Today, Lucy refers to herself as "a mom on a mission," and she's guided by the forceful energy of a single desire:

to prevent others from experiencing the same pain and sorrow of losing their own children. "I lost my son, but I'm still his mother," she says, "and I'll continue to mother him by making sure that I protect the lives of other children like him."

Signs your heat is a mission:

- It's the result of personal, meaningful experience.

- It gives you clarity and direction.

- It makes what is most important in your life impossible to ignore.

INTUITION

Intuition is an internal knowing, a gut feeling that defies logic and overrides your learned responses. It might feel like a knowing when you have to make a hard decision; it could come as a "light bulb" moment when you get a good idea, or it might manifest as the ability to read between the lines. Susan Piver has spent her life listening to her intuition, which she trusts as an inner voice that will always guide her toward her fire. Susan first listened to her intuition in her twenties when she heard the words of a new Bruce Springsteen song on the radio: "There's somethin' happenin' somewhere." To find that something somewhere, Susan's intuition told her to quit her job, pack everything she owned into her car, and drive across the country without a plan. Weeks later, Susan found herself working as a cocktail waitress at a blues bar in Austin. For over a decade, she had a front-row seat to some of the best live music in the world. Eventually, Susan was put in charge of promoting the bar's new record label, another adventure that led her to embark on a career as a music industry executive. And to think, each of those fires in Susan's life was ignited by the lyrics to "Dancing in the Dark." "When I heard Springsteen's words, my life until that moment dissolved, and it showed me a glimmer of the life that could be," Susan says.

Years later, Susan's intuition would lead her to yet another fire as she browsed a Boston bookstore. She found herself drawn to *The Heart of the Buddha*, a book about the teachings of Buddhism by Chögyam Trungpa, a Tibetan meditation master. Suddenly, Susan had an insatiable desire to learn more about Buddhism, and she noticed that every book she bought included a bookmark imprinted with the name of a Buddhist publishing company. Susan's intuition told her to reach out to the company, which is how she ended up befriending the man who became her meditation teacher (and still is, decades later). Today, Susan is an avowed Buddhist and meditation teacher and the leader of the Open Heart Project, an online meditation community of nearly twenty thousand practitioners. "This is how my life has always worked," Susan says. "The world opens a door, creates a coincidence, or puts something in my path that coheres with the wanting."

Signs your heat is intuition:

- You've been led by an unexplainable feeling of knowing.

- You've experienced deep and persistent urges to act.

- You notice signs and sensations that are difficult to ignore.

ANGER

Over the years, the most common form of heat I've seen lead women to find their fire is anger, but it's also the most complicated. There's a societal double standard that requires women to be nurturing, passive, and emotionally controlled while men are allowed—even encouraged—to be aggressive. That's why when women are angry on their own behalf, they're called bitchy, crazy, difficult, or shrill. To avoid that blowback, we learn early on that the only form of anger that's acceptable is turning that heat into benevolent action on behalf of others. As the de facto caretakers of our families and communities, that action is often activism. From prohibition to the water crisis in Flint, Michigan, to the election of Donald Trump, it's women's anger that puts them on the front lines of activism, which, in turn, is often the gateway to finding their fire. That was certainly how it happened for me; the heat I felt after the shooting at Sandy Hook School wasn't just anger but pure, unadulterated rage.

Mimi Rocah's mother was the victim of a violent rape in a parking lot near the hospital where she was a medical student in Chicago in the 1950s; she rarely spoke about the assault except to say that when it happened, no one had supported her. At the time, rape wasn't considered a serious crime, and police hadn't even attempted to locate and arrest her mother's attacker. This injustice, which was imprinted in Mimi's consciousness, so angered her that she went to law school to become a sex crimes prosecutor and help victims like her mother. For more than sixteen years, Mimi did exactly that as a federal prosecutor until—once again—she was motivated by anger to take on another challenge. In 2017, Mimi was so angered by President Trump's critical public comments about key institutions like the DOJ and FBI that she decided to quit her job and run for office. Mimi, who was a Moms Demand Action volunteer at the time, was inspired by the organization's value that big change can happen on a small level. "It reminded me about how important it is to have passionate women in power who will lead with humanity and force change," Mimi says. In 2020, after running a grassroots campaign fueled by the support of Moms Demand Action volunteers, Mimi was elected the district attorney of Westchester County, New York.

Signs your heat is anger:

- It's triggered by injustice.

- It compels you to protect others.

- It's so powerful it makes you want to take action.

LIGHT THE MATCH

Reflect on your past heat moments

Having read the examples of other firestarters' heat, can you think of times when you experienced heat in your life? What did it feel like? Did you act on it, or did you push it down? Now that you've identified your desires and your heat, can you think of how you might cultivate heat in alignment with your current desires?

FAN THE FLAMES

List your longings

In your firestarter journal, make a list of your desires. Nothing is too big or too small. These will help you uncover what you burn for. If you feel stuck, reflect on the desires you had as a child. What did you want when no dream seemed too big? Also, look at the list of firestarters you admire. What desires do you think they are acting on? Do any of those desires resonate with you?

Heat is the core of your fire triangle. It is the very thing that makes you feel alive. It is the spark that ignites your fire. But your goal is not to identify a single source of heat. What ignites your fire today may be different a year from now or even next week. Your goal is to become attuned to the different ways heat rises within you and to practice following that heat toward better and brighter fires. Pay attention to your emotions—especially the ones society tells you to silence—as they are powerful signals. For many firestarters, the heat of their desires is deeply connected to their values. We'll talk more about how to identify your values in the next chapter. For now, remember that heat is your ultimate guide. Trust and follow it, and it will lead you to the next fiery thing.

6

Tapping Into the
Oxygen of Your Values

Your personal values are the ideals you use to judge what is meaningful in your life and what isn't. They're the beliefs and principles shaped by your faith, culture, education, relationships, and personal experiences that help you decide what matters to you and set boundaries around what doesn't. Brené Brown, a researcher who has spent decades studying human emotion, says, "A value is a way of being or believing what we hold most important. Living into our values means that we do more than profess our values, we practice them. We walk our talk. We are clear about what we believe and hold important, and we take care that our intentions, words, thoughts, and behaviors align with those beliefs."[1]

Just like fire needs oxygen to burn, your desires are informed by the values that give your life meaning. Whether you're deciding to make a career change or carve out more space for real self-care, defining and prioritizing your personal values will be a vital part of activating your fire triangle. The alignment of your heat and your values will allow you to sustain the work needed to start and grow your fires past that initial moment of heat when you're buzzing with energy and everything still feels possible.

It wasn't until the Sandy Hook School shooting that my values became clear to me, and looking back, I can see they'd been present my entire life. In grade school, I was fixated on the stories of women like Harriet Tubman, Elizabeth Cady Stanton, and other suffragists and civil rights activists who had lived in or passed through my hometown—women with a moral clarity I wanted to emulate. In high school, I read obsessively about the Watergate scandal, even though the political drama had played out when I was just a toddler. The fallibility of elected officials and the importance of protecting democracy—the very values of America—made me want to become an investigative journalist. Given these formative experiences—all of which called on my core values—it seems obvious in retrospect that I would go on to start Moms Demand Action. And I can't help but wonder what my life might have looked like if I'd identified and lived intentionally in alignment with those values earlier on.

My story is proof that it's never too late to get back on course, even if you feel like you've lost sight of your values. Just like the North Star used to guide explorers home, your values act as the North Star of your fire triangle. They provide a grounding and guiding force for your desires. Below is a list of the values held by many of the firestarters I've interviewed and worked with. As you read through them, ask yourself which values resonate the most with who you are or want to be.

INTEGRITY

If you value your integrity, you're guided by strong and unbending moral principles like trustworthiness, honesty, and transparency, and you're committed to doing the right thing, even when no one is watching. For Rebecca Bauer-Kahan, a descendant of Austrian Jews who were desperate to flee their homeland as Hitler rose to power in Germany, integrity was a matter of life or death. Rebecca's relatives, including her grandmother, were only able to survive the Holocaust after a distant family friend—a stranger—in New York agreed to write a letter sponsoring them to move to America. "Even though this woman didn't know my family, she made a moral choice to help us," says Rebecca. "Her integrity impacted generations of lives, and it taught me about the moral power one person could have."

Now, as a lawyer and lawmaker, Rebecca has tried to pay that integrity forward. When Rebecca was tapped to assist with California's legal response to the Trump administration's Muslim ban, she found herself in the middle of the San Francisco airport waiting for ten refugees to land. The Trump administration wanted to turn them away, but Rebecca knew that if that happened, the refugees' lives would be in danger back at home. The crisis reminded Rebecca of the boats America turned away during the Holocaust, and she was determined to get every last refugee off the plane and bring them to safety. Hours later, Rebecca's legal team prevailed, and the refugees deplaned—a full-circle moment for Rebecca: "I was standing with the mother of a refugee who collapsed with relief when her son deplaned and I thought, 'My God, what one woman once did for me, I just did for someone else.'"

Signs you value integrity:

- You're trustworthy and reliable.

- You take responsibility.

- You have strong moral principles.

COMMUNITY

If you value community, you see significance in a sense of camaraderie and connectedness. You believe we all have an individual role to play in community, but when we come together, we can collectively create even more meaning. That might mean you're committed to raising money for charities, or you're invested in local sports, or you're hosting a block party for your neighbors. You come alive when you're helping your community in some way. Jerri Green says she learned the importance of community growing up in an impoverished family that was poor enough to qualify for assistance for food and shelter. Even though they didn't have a lot, Jerri's father also modeled for her what it meant to take care of your community. "If he caught a lot of fish, he'd take some to a family he knew was in need. If he was out buying Christmas gifts, he'd get a few for the kids he knew wouldn't have much under the tree," Jerri says of her father. "He taught me to find small ways to look out for the needs of my neighbors and do my part to help them out."

Jerri ended up going to Georgetown to become a lawyer, always intending to return home and use her law degree to help her community. After graduating, she worked for Memphis nonprofits and in the mayor's office, where she helped secure legal assistance for people who were in need because they lacked money or were victims of abuse. The more Jerri worked to help her community, the more she realized she could make an even bigger difference if she were elected to office. "I've never been interested in getting a big paycheck or a corner office or fancy title," Jerri says. "For me, it's just, 'How can I help more people?' That's when I feel most alive."

The first time Jerri ran for office, she lost. But she felt so strongly that she needed and deserved to get elected that she ran again . . . and won. Now, Jerri is helping to make and pass policies on everything from immigration to domestic violence. She says the best part of her job is meeting with community members to hear their concerns and then connect them to the help they need. "My community is like my oxygen. Without it, I wouldn't have survived my childhood," says Jerri. "Giving back to my community is what feeds my fire."

Signs you value community:

- You prioritize shared values, beliefs, and goals over your own interests.

- You're open to diverse perspectives.

- You're a problem solver.

LEARNING

If your value is learning, you're committed to gaining new knowledge or skills through experience, practice, observation, or instruction.

You see knowledge as a gateway to wisdom, which can expand both your perspective and your opportunities. You realize learning isn't finite—something that only happens inside schools and universities—but a process that should continue throughout your lifetime and bear fruit in future generations. Anna King's learning journey began when her son started struggling behaviorally in school because he was bored and not challenged enough in the classroom. He was labeled a troublemaker. Anna, the child of a white mother and Black father in Oklahoma, was forced to attend segregated schools in the South and has vivid memories of being bullied by racist students, parents, and teachers. To spare her son the same kind of trauma, Anna made significant sacrifices to advocate for her son to have access to special accommodations to ensure he received a quality education. During the day, Anna was at her son's side in school, and after she put her kids to bed, she worked the night shift.

After years of advocating for her son, Anna learned how to navigate the school system. She learned about all the things that were broken, including a lack of support for students. So when her daughter told her that her high school English class didn't have access to the books they needed, Anna organized a parent coalition to shake the resources loose from the school district. But this time, Anna had to learn a whole new system—not just a classroom, but the Oklahoma City school district. Anna began organizing and training parents to testify at district meetings and studied ways to get the media to cover her campaign. In the end, not only did Anna get the new books for her daughter's classroom, but the principal was so impressed by her savvy that she asked Anna to serve as president of the parent-teacher association. She quickly rose through the ranks.

First, she was elected to lead the PTA for the entire school district in 2009; then, she ran from the floor to become the Oklahoma PTA president. After, she was elected to serve as a National PTA board member and later became the president of the National PTA in 2021. She was only the third person of color to ever hold the position for the National PTA.

Anna dedicated her tenure to making sure that the needs of all children—especially marginalized Black, brown, and Indigenous children—were met. "My grandmother, a descendant of slaves, always told me, 'You have to learn from the past to understand the present and make the future better. The people in your family who went through these things made it possible for you to flourish so you can learn and help others,'" Anna says. While her childhood dream of becoming a civil rights attorney may not have come true, her commitment to making a change did, because public education is a civil rights issue.

Signs you value learning:

- You're constantly seeking knowledge.

- You're comfortable operating outside your comfort zone.

- You approach new things with curiosity.

DIGNITY

If you value dignity, you care about treating others with respect, and you accept others for who they are, even—maybe especially—if they're different from you, or even if you have disagreements. This could mean you're committed to listening to and encouraging others' opinions and input, or you make it a practice to validate other people's contributions, or you stand up to bullies online and in real life. Olivia Julianna describes herself as a Latina from rural Texas, and she has learned to value respect from her own experience of being bullied for her weight. Olivia wasn't just bullied at school; she was also taunted at home. "My family bought my clothes a size too small on purpose," Olivia says. "I can't remember a time in my life when people in my family weren't making comments about my looks."

Olivia sought solace in her school's debate team and began getting involved in local politics, which boosted her confidence and self-esteem. When she was seventeen, she took her public speaking skills to TikTok and posted a video about the presidential election, which quickly went viral. Of course, the double-edged sword of virality is that even as she was getting praise for her political aptitude, the comments section of her video overflowed with cutting remarks about her body, as well as threats to her physical safety. But Olivia wasn't deterred. During one back-and-forth on Twitter about abortion with Florida Congressman Matt Gaetz, the representative attempted to humiliate Olivia by tweeting a photo of her and implying that she was too unattractive to impregnate and therefore didn't have to worry about needing an abortion. Olivia then took to the internet, understandably outraged by Rep. Gaetz's attack on a teen, and harnessed all that attention to raise over $2 million for fifty different abortion funds across the country. Olivia, who's in her twenties now, says the dustup barely fazed her: "In retrospect, I think being bullied so much when I was younger taught me to respect myself, even or especially when others didn't. Maybe it all happened for a reason."

Lawmakers at all levels of government now court Olivia for her help with their elections and political messaging. And Olivia, who dreams of one day running to be the governor of Texas, says the journey from being tormented to being celebrated has taught her the value of self-respect. "I stand up to bullies, and I won't let people talk disrespectfully to me, whether it's someone in my family or a sitting congressman," Olivia says. "I no longer doubt myself. I know what I'm good at, I know what skills I have. I will never again let anyone make me question whether I deserve a seat at the table."

Signs you value dignity:

- You stand up for your beliefs.

- You're comfortable with confrontation.

- You can establish strong boundaries.

EMPATHY

If you value empathy, you see the inherent importance of placing yourself in another person's shoes—you seek out others' perspectives and attempt to identify with their emotions. Empathy is the value that defines our humanity and helps us build strong relationships, foster understanding, and create a more compassionate society. When you cultivate empathy, it can propel you to take action to relieve the suffering of others; it's the value that moves you from feeling to doing. Zoe Winkler Reinis has felt a deep connection to other people's emotions her entire life. When she was eleven years old, her father, the actor Henry Winkler, took her to a local shelter to help feed the unhoused on Thanksgiving Day. Zoe was so overcome by the notion that some people didn't have homes that she began sobbing and inviting people at the shelter over to her home. "I was told to go home because I was upsetting the people who were just there to eat Thanksgiving dinner," Zoe says.

That same deep-seated empathy is what spurred Zoe to act after learning about the impact of the Trump administration's policy of separating immigrant families at the United States–Mexico border. One morning, as she watched the news while getting her three kids ready for school, she saw an image of a mom talking to a border patrol agent as her toddler daughter held on to her leg and cried. "It was as if someone took a cattle brand and stamped that image in my head," Zoe says. "I saw my kids in those kids, and I saw myself in those moms. The only thing that separated us was where we were born."

Signs you value empathy:

- You can relate others' experiences to your own.

- You feel the emotions of others deeply.

- You're an active listener.

COURAGE

Courage is the value of anyone who pushes past their doubts and fears and moves forward with confidence. If you value courage, you are committed to making difficult choices and taking action, even though you know it could be difficult, challenging, and, at times, painful. That might be the courage to say you're sorry, to ask for a raise, or to stand up against injustice. Mallory McMorrow, one of many women across the country who felt compelled to run for office after the 2016 election of Donald Trump, became the youngest woman ever elected to the Michigan state senate. Because she was a young and outspoken woman, Mallory found herself the target of the opposition party. One morning, Mallory woke up to notifications on her phone that a Republican colleague had claimed in a campaign fundraising email that Mallory wanted to "groom" and "sexualize" kindergartners.[2] "As a mother, this was my breaking point," says Mallory, who knew she had to make it clear that her opponents couldn't say whatever they wanted without consequences.

Mallory spent an entire night writing a speech about the email to give on the floor and then spent her ninety-minute commute from her home in Lansing rehearsing it in the car. She had a feeling it would resonate with others who were fed up with conspiracy theories, and she was right. Mallory's speech, which lasted just four minutes and forty seconds, was a fierce and impassioned call to come together in the face of challenges and look for solutions instead of blaming people who have been othered as the cause of the issue: "We cannot let hateful people tell you otherwise, to scapegoat and deflect from the fact that they are not doing anything to fix the real issues that impact people's lives. And I know that hate will only win if people like me stand by and let it happen," Mallory said.

As soon as Mallory posted her speech online, it went viral, garnering over one million views in just a few hours, along with a call from President Biden. Seemingly overnight, Mallory's courage to stand up on behalf of people who were marginalized made her a household name. And even though she was on the receiving end of a fire hose of hate, including threats of death and sexual violence, they were far outweighed by the letters she got in her PO box for months from people all over the world telling her how much her speech meant to them. "There's privilege in being able to use my position to help people who are regularly under attack, who don't have the same protections I do, and who are in real danger if people like me don't take the hit and try to push back," Mallory says.

Signs you value courage:

- You speak up for your beliefs.

- You're not afraid to take an unpopular stand.

- You're able to keep going even in the most difficult circumstances.

LIGHT THE MATCH

List how you live your values

In your firestarter journal, list the values that have been most important to you in your life, along with examples of times you've embodied those values. Think back to the times in your life when you were pushed to act: What makes you angry? What breaks your heart? What fills you with joy?

Though heat is the core of your fire triangle, it is your values that sustain the energy heat provides. Values are what nurture and strengthen your desires. They act as a compass that steers you toward not just meaningful actions but also an authentic, intentional life. This alignment of values and desires is the essence of living on fire—a state where your actions are driven by a profound sense of authenticity and conviction.

Just as values give meaning and direction to your heat, your abilities are what allow your fire to grow. In the next chapter we'll explore how recognizing and cultivating your abilities can strengthen your fire and empower you to live your values in a bigger and brighter way than you have before. But it is important to remember that values are what ground your fire's growth. By remaining true to your values even when you begin to attain traditional markers of success like money and status, you ensure that you are building not just a fiery life but a life that lets you burn.

Like heat, these values will evolve over time. Life experiences, personal growth, changing political landscapes, and new environments will continuously reshape what you hold dear. Embrace this evolution and practice checking in with yourself. Keep your values close, let them ground you, and watch how they enrich your life.

7

Adding the Fuel
of Your Abilities

In real-life fires, kindling like dry grass and sticks is what helps transform a fire from a small flame to a full-out blaze. And in order to keep a fire growing and going, that kindling has to be added on a regular basis or it will die out. For your fire triangle, consider your kindling all your innate and acquired gifts, talents, and skills; they're the natural and distinctive ways you see or do things that, combined with all the knowledge you've acquired during your life, make you uniquely you.

Time and time again, I've witnessed women deny and downplay their abilities. Because society doesn't encourage women to show off their strengths, you might be reading this and wondering whether you have any unique gifts or skills—if that's the case, I promise you they're hiding in plain sight. It's often easy to overlook the things that come naturally to you. It could be something as simple as the way you capture an image with a camera, or how you keep the trains running at work or at home, or how you make people feel like you're really listening when they talk to you. Every gift, talent, or skill you possess—no matter how small or inconsequential it may seem to you—will help you start a fire that is authentic and meaningful to you. Here are some of the broad abilities that many women possess but often don't recognize or claim.

CONNECTING

If you're a connector, you're committed to investing time, energy, and attention into the relationships that nourish and strengthen you. You understand that getting outside your comfort zone and seeking out strangers will make you healthier, mentally and physically. But connecting can also help you live on fire by encouraging meaningful conversations that lead to new ideas or interactions. For some people, connecting is totally intuitive; for others who might be more introverted or shy, connecting might seem like a terrifying proposition. But don't underplay your ability to connect; if you belong to a book club or you volunteer or you attend a place of worship, you might already be connecting without realizing it.

Susan McPherson's origins as a serial connector started at her childhood breakfast table in Latham, New York, where every morning her parents spread out five national and local newspapers and clipped every article that could be of interest to someone they knew. Then they would each go to their respective manual typewriter, type up a short note to accompany each article, and put them all in the mail. "I thought everybody's parents did this," says Susan, an only child. "But now I realize what they were doing was very special. They were connecting with intentionality, and it made me want to do the same."

Years later, when Susan got her first fax machine in the late 1980s, she realized technology could help her do what her parents had done with newspapers much more efficiently. And then, with the advent of email, LinkedIn, and Facebook, Susan was able to connect to even more people, and also to connect them to one another. Susan, then a marketing executive, began to get a reputation as a connector, but it wasn't until a girls' trip that she realized her talent was unique. "My girlfriends and I had a goal to come up with elevator speeches about ourselves to use as bios on social media," Susan says. "I said, 'I'm Susan McPherson, and I'm a serial connector.' At first I was embarrassed because it sounded so ridiculous, but as soon as I articulated my burning desire, I felt powerful."

It was after that trip that Susan decided to create her own communications company focused on connecting people, and she also began writing a book about it, called *The Lost Art of Connecting: The Gather, Ask, Do Method for Building Meaningful Relationships*. That book, which came out during the pandemic, provided a lifeline to many people struggling with isolation and loneliness. Susan says she now realizes her mission in life is to show and teach people about the power of connecting, not just in their careers but in their personal lives. "Every morning, I still reach out to three or four people to see how they are doing," Susan says. "You put joy out into the world when you let people know you're thinking about them. And that's what lights me up."

Signs you're a connector:

- You belong to many varied communities.

- Meeting and introducing people energizes you.

- You're able to nurture many relationships at a time.

CREATIVITY

Creativity isn't just about being artistic; it's the ability to express yourself in new ways, including problem-solving, coming up with fresh ideas, or finding innovative methods for doing something. If you've ever been in a brainstorm or made a vision board, you've tapped into your creativity. If you've found a new way to entertain your kids, or added your own flair to a recipe, or helped spruce up a community space for others to enjoy, you've been creative. Fostering that creativity can help you live on fire by creating more openings and opportunities for inspiration.

Bridgette Sloan was born into a family of creative women in Columbus, Ohio, where she was one of four children born to an impoverished single mother in the projects. But when Bridgette looks back on her childhood, she doesn't remember the struggles as much as the sewing. Her mother, grandmother, and sisters were all seamstresses who had side businesses sewing and mending for local families. Bridgette saw them creating and wanted to join in. "I talked my mother into buying me a Singer hand-crank sewing machine," Bridgette says. "If she was making a ball gown, I'd use her scraps to sew outfits for my Barbie dolls."

Bridgette's mother recognized her talent early on and enrolled her in a sewing class that led her to sew and crochet all her clothes throughout high school. "That one class sparked something in me," Bridgette says. "It made me realize design was my bent in life, and that my creativity could become my career."

Bridgette did go on to get her bachelor's and master's degrees in fashion design—an endeavor that took her nearly twenty years— but she was forced to keep deferring her dream of a career in design to focus on jobs that would support her four children. Finally, when Bridgette retired, she reignited her creative spark and started a store on Etsy selling handmade satin-lined hats specifically designed to protect Black hair. Bridgette's hats are so popular with customers all over the world that she hopes to expand her store and hire staff. "Sometimes I wonder if I'm too old, but I still get inspired," says Bridgette, who's now in her sixties. "My whole life, it's been, 'Bridgette's not able to do what she wants to do.' Finally I started thinking outside the box. And this time in my life is for me." Soon after realizing this, Bridgette was chosen to feature ten of her apparel designs at the Poised and Proper Fall Fashion Show in Charleston, South Carolina, an event celebrating designers and models who are mothers.

Signs you're a creator:

- You're informed and inspired by new trends.

- You like to apply new ideas and approaches to problem-solving.

- You view your life as a form of self-expression.

LEADERSHIP

Think of leadership as having two flavors. Leadership with an uppercase "L" is the person who's comfortable in front of any audience, who likes taking the reins, and who is a big-picture thinker. Leadership with a lowercase "l" is about the decisions you make in your everyday life, and it's just as much of an ability as the uppercase kind. Even the influence you have in your life as a woman or mother is a form of leadership. If you're in charge of making decisions about where your kids go to school and what doctors they see, you're a leader. If you're taking care of your aging parents, you're a leader. If you oversee all the schedules in your household, you're a leader. Every day, you're making decisions that affect others' lives and your own, and people see you as a leader, whether you know it or not.

Roseann Stanley, a self-described introvert who feared public speaking her whole life, never viewed herself as a leader until she retired and started going online to share her political views. Roseann was a novice, but found the more she posted to social media platforms like Twitter, the more followers she had who were interested in her political viewpoints. Despite her fears of public speaking, Roseann followed the suggestion of one of her followers who told her she should host weekly online conversations about political issues. At first, only a dozen or so people joined Roseann's forums, but soon, thousands were tuning in to listen and learn from her. Those online interactions gave Roseann the confidence to start volunteering offline with organizations like Moms Demand Action, and she also began teaching others how to phone and text bank for political issues and elections. By the time a county commission seat opened up in Roseann's area of town, she felt emboldened to run. "No one else stepped up, so I decided, 'Why not me?'" says Roseann, who didn't win, but found the experience was so exhilarating that she plans to run again next election cycle.

Signs you're a leader:

- You're willing to challenge the status quo.

- You're accountable for your actions.

- You inspire and empower others.

OPTIMISM

Optimism is often seen as an inherent trait, something you're born with, but research shows it's also a skill that can be developed and improved over time. If you're optimistic, you know maintaining a hopeful and positive outlook on life—even in the face of adversity—will make you feel more in control of every situation. That doesn't mean you see the world through rose-colored glasses; you simply choose positivity over pessimism, learn from difficult situations instead of taking disappointments personally, and choose to see the inevitable challenges you'll encounter as new opportunities.

While Mandana Dayani was on maternity leave after the birth of her second daughter, she found herself watching wall-to-wall, gut-wrenching television coverage of families being separated at the United States–Mexico border. It reminded her of her own experience as a religious refugee who fled Iran for the United States as a child. "I was raised with this belief that America saved our lives," Mandana says. "We were always aware of what our lives could have been like, and we felt a responsibility to make the best of our opportunity to live the American dream. When I saw children being ripped away from their parents, I couldn't understand how the country that saved my life could do this to other families. I knew something was broken and was desperate to find an avenue to channel my outrage into positive action."

Mandana, who was raised in Los Angeles, got on a plane to Tornillo, Texas, to visit the first camp housing the separated families. Once she saw it for herself, she knew she had to do everything she could. She reached out to members of Congress to see how she could get involved. "Every single conversation kept going back to, 'If you want to create lasting change, then you need to get more people to vote,'" Mandana says. "And then I just had that *Legally Blonde* 'What, like it's hard?' moment. I mean, if my friends and I could get millions of people excited about a new mascara or Marvel film, how could we not figure out a way to inspire them to show up at the polls?"

Mandana, in partnership with the Creative Artists Agency Foundation, gathered dozens of women leaders in the fashion, entertainment, and tech industries to help launch I Am a Voter, a nonpartisan organization that harnesses the power of content, influencers, and social media to inspire civic participation. To date, the organization's campaigns have helped over half a million people register to vote and have garnered billions of impressions.

Mandana's goal with I Am a Voter is to make voting an integral part of an American's identity, but also to make voting inclusive and aspirational, and to demonstrate how much power we can have—individually and collectively—when we show up. "I am a relentless optimist and a proud American," Mandana says. "I've seen firsthand how—unlike other countries—America provides an incredible, equalizing power to participate in the process. My goal is to focus on what unites us and to inspire others to show up and advocate for their rights. And the ballot box is one of the most powerful ways to do that."

That optimism has been passed down to Mandana's daughter. The pair were invited to the White House Hanukkah party in 2022, and Mandana's then eight-year-old daughter, Anderson, asked President Biden a question on the stage. She asked him for his advice on how she could run for president one day and "help make the world a better place." "That moment was the culmination of my identity as both a refugee and an activist," Mandana says. "I fled my country because it wasn't safe to be Jewish. I had barely any rights as a woman. Now I'm at the White House and my daughter is telling the president of the free world that she wants to be president. I have such hope for the future."

Signs you're an optimist:

- You're energized by challenges.

- You believe you can make difficult situations better.

- You're not easily discouraged.

COMMUNICATION

We've all met people who seem like born communicators—they can effortlessly tell a compelling story or clearly convey an idea.

But communicating is literally just sending or receiving information, and with practice, anyone can become an engaging and authentic communicator. If you're an interested listener, if you're open and honest, if you know your narrative, you're communicating. And the reason communicating is so important to living on fire is that once you learn the skills, you will start to think, "How can I communicate better with my partner? Or with my colleagues? Or even in my own thoughts?" And you might finally start to feel heard.

In retrospect, Samara Bay says, the first time she realized the power of storytelling was when her parents took her to her first Shakespeare play at an outdoor theater in a Northern California redwood forest. As the Bay Area fog rolled in around the actors putting on a modern-day rendition of *The Winter's Tale*, Samara, who was ten years old, sat transfixed. "I thought, I don't even know what this is, but I want it," Samara says. "The power of story and cracking yourself open seemed so exciting, and it connected to all my spark points. It took me a long time to realize that the magic of that night wasn't calling me to be an actor but a storyteller."

Samara spent years trying to find her place in Hollywood as both an actor and a dialect coach. While she was working on the set of *Wonder Woman 1984* in Washington, DC, she got a call that she says was "the spark that made everything else until that moment make sense." MoveOn, a policy advocacy group, wanted Samara to help them coach first-time female candidates running for political office. "We were two years into Donald Trump's term and hurtling toward the midterms, and I was wondering what I could possibly do to be useful beyond going to marches and writing postcards," Samara says. "Training women to run for office was an opportunity to use my skills to help change the narrative in the nation."

Samara started training the women in everything from how to ask for donations to how to tell their personal stories on the stump. She quickly figured out that many of the women who were running didn't think they had a story to tell, or at least not one that was worthy of sharing. "I told them that their story didn't have to have a massive beginning, middle, and end," Samara says. "What we love as humans is hearing when somebody felt like they were in a really tough spot and what they did next. And as these women realized, 'Oh, my small story is good enough,' it tapped into the revolution inside that thought: If we all believe our weird small stories are good enough, it will change the world."

Samara has since written *Permission to Speak: How to Change What Power Sounds Like, Starting with You,* a book about the dissonance between how many people—women, people of color, immigrants, and queer folks—speak versus how we collectively think powerful people—wealthy white men who've historically been in charge—should speak. "I've seen firsthand that when women start to open up—when they stop hiding and embrace who they are and what makes them who they are—there's a change in what power sounds like and, in turn, who has it," Samara says. "That is why I'm in this work."

Signs you're a communicator:

- You're authentic and relatable.

- You're empathetic and in tune with your audience.

- You're not just a clear speaker but a talented listener.

PERSEVERANCE

Perseverance is the ability to keep trying despite obstacles or difficulties—maybe to reach a career goal, but also to stay focused on your own personal growth. You might be determined to overcome a fear, or to take care of yourself despite all the things piling up on your plate, or to change your approach when your plans don't work out as expected. It's a mindset of resilience, determination, and a willingness to learn from failure, and people who persevere keep going—no matter what. For Andrea Hunley, that meant achieving her goals even when people told her she couldn't or shouldn't. The first time that happened was when Andrea was fourteen; she had convinced her parents to let her work in a local yogurt shop. Its owners, a married couple from Ghana, took Andrea under their wing. For years the couple tried to talk Andrea out of her dream of becoming a teacher, advising her to go into law or medicine instead, fields they thought were more prestigious. Andrea says they unwittingly gave her the confidence to stand up for herself. "I had to find it within myself to say to adults, 'I want to be a teacher. This is important to me,'" Andrea says. "It lit a fire and made me even more resolute: I would be a teacher and a damn good one."

Andrea did become a teacher, and by the time she was twenty-six, she was already an elementary school principal. But she knew she wanted an even bigger role that would let her be involved in making Indiana's education policy. When Andrea's state senate district was redrawn and there was no incumbent to run against, she felt it was a sign. "I thought, 'Well. Look at God. I think I've got to run,'" Andrea says. But when she started calling local leaders for their support, they told her she shouldn't run, it wasn't her turn, or it would be too hard for her to win. "I was like, 'White guy hard or Black girl hard?' Because I've only ever known hard," she says. "Being told I couldn't do it was why I had to run."

Andrea ran and won, and she is now one of only five Black lawmakers and one of a handful of lawmakers with school-aged children in the Indiana Senate. She credits her new career in politics to her perseverance. "As a nerdy, biracial girl, I had no choice but to be persistent and determined," Andrea says. "My life has required a level of 'stick-to-itiveness' that I had to dig deep for. And if I ever feel like someone's doubting me for even a second, I'm always ready to fight for what I want."

Though running Moms Demand Action would eventually call upon every one of my skills, I was unaware of how to use those abilities when I drove home from yoga still reeling with rage and hurt after the shooting at Sandy Hook. The funny thing is, I tapped into those skills anyway. Because of my work in crisis PR, communication and management were second nature. It didn't seem remarkable to me then that I made a Facebook group, wrote a compelling post, and loosely implied that I would organize a march on Washington. In the moment, all of that just seemed like something I could do, but now I see it was my abilities coming into alignment with my values.

Signs you're perseverant:

- You view frustration as part of the process, not a roadblock.

- You apply learnings from past failures to new situations.

- You're resilient amid setbacks.

When you think about what skills you have, I want you to think about the things you assume about yourself. I hear so many women say things like "I'm organized because I have to be," or "Somebody has got to do it, might as well be me," or "I'll sleep when I'm dead." But what I hear in those phrases is "I'm organized and detail-oriented," "I'm a leader," "I persevere"—valuable skills that include all your tasks and responsibilities for work, your family, yourself, and your friends. Maybe you're the parent who counsels your child after a tough day at school. Maybe you're the friend everyone goes to when they need a pep talk. Maybe you're the coworker who remembers to get a plan B ready in case plan A falls through. Maybe you've never imagined that these everyday interactions are actually special skills or talents, but identifying and honing those abilities will provide the kindling you need to fuel your personal fire.

FAN THE FLAMES

Audit your weekly tasks

Similar to the time audit you completed earlier, this is an audit of all the tasks you do each week. Using the list you started above, rate how energized and how engaged you were while doing each task. Which task ranks the highest and why? More likely than not, you have some natural talent in that area—maybe you're a good listener or a next-level organizer—but, more important, your high engagement and energy levels mean you're likely to enjoy doing and improving the skill this task requires.

Gather outside input

Poll your friends, family, and coworkers about what they think your strongest abilities are. What do you think of their answers? Did they surprise you? Why or why not? Which skills are the overwhelming winners? Are there ways to utilize those skills in service of your fire?

Whether it's the power to connect, creativity, leadership, optimism, communication, or perseverance, these abilities are the tools that turn your desires and values into real, tangible actions. They are the fuel that ignites and will sustain your fire. And like your desires and your values, your abilities will grow and adapt as you move through life. Living on fire isn't just about utilizing the abilities you have; it's about growing your talents and seeking out fresh skills that will give you the capacity to start fires in your life. This is one of the most exciting parts of starting to live on fire. I've watched firestarter after firestarter grow more confident as she builds new skills and discovers untapped talents. Once women recognize gifts they have, they also realize no one can take those gifts away from them. That understanding comes with a swaggering, unshakable confidence. It is exactly the type of confidence you need to build your fire and release it into the world.

8

Bringing It All Together

Once you've identified your heat (the energy of the desires that motivate you), your oxygen (the values that guide you), and your fuel (the abilities that make you special), you'll need to start practicing different ways to bring all those elements into alignment and ignite your first fire (or maybe just the first fire you've started on purpose). How you do this will be unique to you, but like any practice, aligning your fire triangle will require courage, work, patience, and repetition.

After landing her dream job at CNN as a White House reporter, Jessica Yellin realized she had a talent for translating policy, but she didn't enjoy getting mired in partisan politics. What she really wanted to do was find a way to combine her abilities as a journalist, her values of integrity and honesty in reporting, and her burning desire to help women understand how the policies made by lawmakers influence their lives. Eventually, Jessica left CNN to create an organization focused on fixing what was broken in the news.

But when she presented her idea of creating a women-centered news agency to a myriad of (mostly male) investors, media executives, producers, and venture capitalists, she was repeatedly turned down for funding or partnership.

Frustrated, Jessica decided to go straight to the source: her small audience on Instagram. At the time, she had only nine hundred followers on the platform and videos weren't yet ubiquitous on social media, but she decided to record herself explaining a breaking news story and then posted it to her Instagram page. That was the catalyst that transformed Jessica's Instagram into a news feed and turned her into a trusted media resource with more than one million followers. "In my previous career, I always had this strange dissonance feeling where who I was inside didn't match what I was doing and how I was living outside. I was stuck in the system until I finally followed the fire that told me I needed to do this," Jessica says. "And after I made that first post, women started showing up in droves to support me." After the 2024 election, her phone started blowing up with messages from producers, media executives, investors, and others who said they now saw it—the news really was broken—and asked for her leadership on finding a new path.

Margo Price, a country singer in Nashville, started her fire with a list. Margo's music was fueled by her artistic abilities. Her lyrics were inspired by her values as an activist, and she had a burning desire to become a singer-songwriter, but after several years of singing at open mic nights and sitting in with bands at bars, Margo's music career still wasn't catching fire. One day, while reading the entertainment section of the local newspaper, Margo was inspired to list all the venues she dreamed of playing at in town. She started with the smallest bars, then the larger rock clubs, and at the top of her list was the legendary Ryman Auditorium. Then she showed up at the first bar on her list and convinced the owner to let her perform. Each gig she got opened the door to the next venue on her list. "Everything just started to click into place, and it was like a miracle," says Margo, now a Grammy nominee who has since headlined sold-out shows at the Ryman Auditorium.

My fire started with a press release. After I posted to Facebook about the need for women and mothers to rise up against the gun industry, I took the tens of thousands of likes and comments that poured in from people across the world as confirmation that I was onto something. There was clearly a pent-up demand for change, and I had a feeling I was the right person to turn that energy into action. My fire triangle was primed: I had a burning desire to stop gun violence, I valued the safety of children, and I'd spent decades learning how to create messaging and brands that compelled people to act—I just needed to release that energy out into the world.

Given my background in communications, I gravitated toward what I knew how to do best—I drafted a press release that clarified my intentions: It required me to give my new organization a name, it forced me to succinctly summarize what the new organization would do, it allowed me to name myself as the leader, and it crystallized my clarion call to action for like-minded women across the country to bring their desires, values, and abilities to the table, too. Just as I had done so many times during my career, I uploaded my press release to the wire, sent it out into the world, and waited for the response. Within hours, I was getting inquiries from reporters along with calls, emails, and direct messages from dozens of women who had also decided it was time to get off the sidelines and fight for gun safety. They saw that I was fired up and serious about taking action, which gave them permission to do the same. Writing and distributing that press release did more than just promote my new organization—it ignited my fire *and* enlisted like-minded women to help me grow it.

Now it's time for you to practice aligning your fire triangle in whatever way works best for you. You've already taken a big and important first step toward becoming a firestarter by identifying the components of your unique fire triangle. The next step is releasing that energy out into the world to start a fire.

FAN THE FLAMES

Make an announcement

Write your own post, list, or press release describing your fire and get feedback from your friends and family. When I was working in public relations, I came up with this formula for promoting a product or person. Answer these questions and prompts while writing your press release, and you'll come up with a succinct way to describe your fire:

- What is your goal?

- Why should someone listen to you?

- What is the unmet need?

- What is your solution?

- Provide three data points.

- Tell your audience what you want them to do.

WHERE THERE'S SMOKE, THERE'S FIRE

Once you put your fire out into the world, you'll find that you start to uncover parts of yourself that you didn't know existed. You'll begin to evolve in ways you never expected. These are the beneficial side effects of your fire—you thought your fire was focused on one specific outcome, but suddenly, you realize there are all these other unexpected and tangential benefits of going after what you want. Maybe you're more vocal at work, or maybe you're more willing to have tough conversations with family, or maybe you're more clear about your personal boundaries. Whatever the changes are for you, your fire will turn you from a bystander in your life to an active participant, and fuel you with the confidence to be bolder in all aspects of your life.

Before starting Moms Demand Action, I was petrified of public speaking. If I'm being honest, I might not have published my Facebook page if someone had told me that just a few weeks later I'd be required to deliver remarks to hundreds of people at a rally in Washington, DC. After trying everything possible to get out of speaking, I forced myself to show up. Backstage in the greenroom, I was literally green. The closer it got to my turn to go out onstage, the more violently I shook with fear. When I was finally introduced, I kept my eyes down and hurried through my speech, reading every word verbatim and without inflection. Minutes later, still looking at the ground, I sprinted back inside.

I was no Amanda Gorman, but the requests to speak kept coming in. It was clear that public speaking would be part of the activist job description; there was no way to escape it. But something interesting started to happen. Ten speeches later, I got comfortable enough to ad-lib some lines. Twenty speeches later, I was bold enough to look around the room and make eye contact with people in the audience. Hundreds of speeches later, I was so grounded in what I knew and how to say it that I could speak to crowds of thousands off-the-cuff without fear. The more I spoke in public, the better I got at it; the better I got, the more I wanted to do it. And then I found myself using that new and authoritative stage voice in real life, too. Even though I'd always considered myself an introvert, my growth as a speaker encouraged me to stand up to the online trolls who tried to tear me down the moment I started Moms Demand Action. Gun extremists assumed they'd be able to silence me, but I was newly emboldened to take on (and take down) the trolls. And in my personal life, I started standing up for myself more, too. When conservative family members criticized me for starting an organization that they claimed would undermine their gun rights, I was armed with the facts. Instead of backing down like the old me might have done, I felt empowered to debate them.

Overcoming my fear of public speaking didn't just make me a better speaker; the confidence I gained from not giving up and finding my voice showed up in other parts of my life. And that's the profound thing that happens to women who live on fire. Like Gretchen Carlson, whose childhood experience standing up to bullies helped her stand up to men who were harassing her at Fox News. Or Zoe Winkler Reinis, who says activism helped her overcome feelings of inferiority due to her dyslexia and made it easier for her to have difficult conversations about polarizing issues. Or Lisa Ling, whose passion for telling the stories of marginalized people helped her overcome her imposter syndrome by pushing her into spaces Asian American women had never been invited into. Or Julie Bogart, founder of Brave Writer, who was finally able to admit she wanted to go to graduate school in her forties and went for it just because she wanted to, without excuses or apologies. "After presenting my thesis, I remember walking out of that room thinking it was the most satisfying experience of my life, even more than giving birth," Julie says. "It was an experience that was just for me."

Or Monica Molenaar, who signed up for an African dance class, the first dance performance class she'd ever taken, to challenge her fear of trying new things and being on stage. Not only did the class lead Monica to travel through Africa, but it gave her a newfound sense of confidence. "My worry that people might judge me always held me back until that dance class," Monica says. "I put something out into the world that I knew wouldn't be perfect, but I was proud of it anyway, and that helped me see I could survive uncomfortable situations and come out stronger."

Like all these women, your fire will lead you to start living with more intention and confidence. As you build your fire, don't just celebrate the ways you grow that relate to your fire (like getting physically stronger if you want to get fit or becoming a better writer if you have dreams of being a journalist). Make sure to celebrate the ways you are growing as a person, like becoming more confident or more courageous. These personal developments are just as, if not more, important than the growth of any individual fire. This personal work is why living on fire is a lifelong practice. Each fire teaches us new things about ourselves. Each fire reveals new skills, values, and desires. No matter what fire you end up starting, the risks you take to nurture and grow its flames will make you a stronger, more confident, and more *you* you.

LIGHT THE MATCH

How have you grown?

In your firestarter journal, reflect on the ways you've grown since starting your fire. Did you grow in the ways you expected? Do the people closest to you, or the people on your firestarter team, notice how you've changed? How else do you hope to grow?

PART THREE

Sustaining Your Fire

A few weeks after starting Moms Demand Action, while sitting at my kitchen table attempting to help my kids with their homework, write legislative testimony, and listen in to my sixth conference call of the day, I felt a rising sense of panic. The fear started in my stomach and moved up into my chest, pinning me to my seat. I was both cold and hot; my fingers and toes tingled, and I was sweating even though it was a cold winter day. The feeling was frightening but also familiar; it was the same angst that had percolated inside me for so long before it finally spilled over in Dr. Miller's office all those years ago. This time, though, I knew exactly what was causing it.

Seemingly overnight, I'd gone from a stay-at-home mom of five to a gun safety "expert." I was overwhelmed by the threats my family was getting from gun extremists, and I was sleep-deprived by the endless, all-consuming workload I'd taken on. From the moment I woke up, I was on calls or in meetings, and each night, I worked until long after everyone else in my house was asleep. Instead of driving my kids to their extracurriculars and enjoying relaxing dinners where we would unwind and talk about our days, I was either holed up in a room with my laptop or I was on the road. Add to that the pressure of learning the ins and outs of a new, complex issue while managing hundreds of volunteers and begging for money to keep the organization afloat.

All that pressure had been mounting, and suddenly, I was reconsidering whether I wanted to finish what I'd started. While I couldn't stand the thought of living in a world where children weren't safe in their schools and communities, I also wasn't sure if I could withstand the toll my new mission was taking on my mental health.

I went into my closet, lay down on the floor, and cried for a few minutes—something that had become a daily ritual. Just as I was working myself up into heaving sobs, my cell phone rang. "Probably another call from a gun nut," I thought, but on the screen was the name of a woman I'd worked with years ago in public relations. Sheryl and I weren't close friends, but I had always respected her and valued her opinion. All these years later, I still have no idea why Sheryl was calling me that day, because I immediately hijacked her call with my own concerns.

I answered the phone, still in tears, and Sheryl, who I'm sure was both concerned and confused, listened patiently and empathetically as I attempted to ask her the question that had been fueling my panic: "Do I have to do this?" Without asking me for any clarifying context, Sheryl calmly and firmly said, "Shannon, you don't have to do anything you don't want to do. You have every right to go back to your normal life. You have to do what is best for you and for your family. And if that means Moms Demand Action doesn't happen, that's okay."

Those four sentences were exactly what I needed to hear, even though they were from a practical stranger. The ever-present fear I'd felt eased, and the ball of anxiety in my stomach and chest released. I exhaled deeply. It was as if Sheryl's words had opened a pressure valve, and without the fog of fear, I could see clearly that I was at yet another crossroads in my life; I had to choose whether to double down or back down. And in that instant, I knew I wanted to keep going; I wanted to grow the fire I had started. It was my fire, dammit, and I wasn't going to let anyone else put it out.

9

Keeping the Flames Alive

Moms Demand Action is now so large and so formidable that it's laughable to think that it was once so vulnerable and that its future hinged on a call from someone I barely knew. But that was just one of many more inflection points to come; along the way, I was continually presented with the choice to let the fire I started die out, or give it more air and more fuel to make it burn bigger and brighter.

I could have stepped back after my first Facebook post when I started getting threats from extremists; instead, I put out a press release that led to media attention, which led to calls from women offering me their support and skills. In early 2013, after the federal legislation we were trying to pass failed in the Senate, I could have decided the country wasn't ready for change; instead, I turned the organization's focus to changing laws at the state level. When I was ready to put out my own fire, to step back from my leadership position at the organization, I could have tried to burn the whole thing down; instead, I handed the baton over to another leader. And now, in retrospect, I can see that Moms Demand Action is the culmination of all those decisions to keep stoking the flames, over and over again.

These will be the choices you face, too. Starting a fire is an action; living on fire is a way of life. It's the difference between doing and being. Living on fire means you are acting with intention and authenticity—no matter how high the stakes or how scary the risks you are taking might be, you make the choice to forge ahead because it is what you want. Growing your fire is how you grow yourself, and growing yourself is how you grow your fires. It's a lifelong, never-ending process of change that will lead you down many incredible paths and into the lives of amazing people. This growth will be a testament—to yourself and others—that you are committed to prioritizing your own fulfillment, but it won't be without its challenges. Growth is built through change, and that change rarely comes without discomfort. It's that discomfort that makes growing your fire so challenging and is why so many women struggle, get stuck, or even surrender at this stage in the process.

Over and over again, I've watched women start fires in their lives—from learning a new skill to going to therapy to setting up new businesses to walking away from a relationship that no longer serves them—only to abandon it when faced with what it will take to grow it. You might understandably begin to wonder, "What if I can't sustain this? What if it consumes me? What if the fire I built burns out of control?" Having almost abandoned Moms Demand Action many times along the way, I completely understand the daunting feeling that maybe growing your fire is too much or too hard. But the truth is, that discomfort is a sign that you're on the right track. While recognizing that won't necessarily make the process easier, it will give you the power and the opportunity to prepare yourself for whatever comes next.

THE MESSY MIDDLE

After you've built your fire, there will come a time when you realize it's going to take so much more to get to where you're going than you originally imagined. This is what's called the messy middle. Brené Brown refers to the messy middle as the part of a process when we find "we're in the dark, the doors close behind us, we're too far in to turn around and not close enough to the end to see the light." But, Brené also observes, "the middle is messy, but it's also where all the magic happens, all the tension that creates goodness and learning."[1] The liminal space that exists between what was before you started your fire and what's to come will feel frustrating; the progress you're making might feel slow and incremental, which will lead to doubts and frustrations. Suddenly, the excitement that was there when you built your fire might be overcome by feelings of tiredness, vulnerability, and uncertainty. You might start to think about turning back or speeding through this period of transformation, but the messy middle is the most interesting and fruitful place to be, filled with opportunities to expand your perspective and to challenge and stretch yourself.

Sara Smirin applied to Harvard Divinity School when she was fifty-five years old, ten years after she'd walked out of her job the day of the Sandy Hook School shooting and ended up helping me get Moms Demand Action off the ground. After spending years training thousands of volunteers across the country to become activists, Sara felt pulled to further her education and to study how activism, not unlike religion or spirituality, can be transformative. But when the program started, Sara quickly realized it was going to be much more intense than she'd expected, from an immediate, deep immersion into concepts she wasn't familiar with, to taking tests and writing papers every week. Sara says while she was in this messy middle, she wondered how she'd make it to the end. But she was able to push through by leaning on the lessons she learned as a Moms Demand Action leader, including reaching out to students in her cohort for help, asking family and friends for encouragement when she felt overwhelmed, and letting go of her own judgment about her performance. "Activism taught me not to let perfect be the enemy of good, so I'm trying to focus on what I learn, not my letter grades," Sara says. "And I'm staying open, which is how the biggest, most impactful periods of my life have unfolded in the past."

Even the toughest firestarters can be shaken by the overwhelming feeling that everything is happening all at once when they get to the messy middle. During the more challenging stages of growing and sustaining your fire, you might feel the same rising sense of panic I did in those early days of Moms Demand Action. Some days, you might face logistical issues, like losing funding or being understaffed for an important event. Another day, you might have to deal with unsupportive friends or rejection or long hours of unrecognized work. On yet another day, you might have to balance a family crisis with trying to grow your fire. The most successful firestarters weather the storm by relying on three key tactics that we'll discuss in the next chapter: finding strength, staying positive, and gathering support. Honing these skills is how firestarters don't just survive the messy middle, but thrive in the face of constant change.

10

Tools to Sustain Your Fire

n the early days of Moms Demand Action, when I was spending a little too much time curled up in my closet, seemingly every day brought a new challenge that knocked me back to square one. It felt like the skills I'd fought to master the day before all but flew out the window when a new, totally different challenge landed on my desk the next morning. Most days, I found the resolve to tackle the process all over again, but other days ended in tears. It was truly trial by fire.

What I learned in that process was that although the problems changed day to day, even hour to hour, how I helped myself get through them did not. No matter what obstacle stood in my way, I fell back on these three tools. I faked my confidence until I felt it, I radiated positivity, and I gathered and leaned on supportive people. These practices, which we'll discuss in depth in this chapter, didn't offer me specific strategies for how to navigate bureaucracy or fundraise under pressure. What these tools provided me was a way to feed my spirit and strengthen my resilience, so I felt ready to take on any challenge—no matter how daunting. And when I began to interview other firestarters for this book, I wasn't surprised to learn that they used the same tools, even though their fires were radically different from mine.

Both building an individual fire and committing to living a life on fire are messy, unpredictable journeys. There's no such thing as linear progress when you are a firestarter. At first, living on fire will likely feel like everything is happening at once. It's exciting, but also overwhelming. You'll need to learn how to find your strength, stay positive, and create your own support system to navigate through the wild and unpredictable messy middle. But, like everything in your firestarter journey, this guidance only works if you turn it into a practice.

FAKE IT TILL YOU MAKE IT

Becoming confident is all about stepping into the version of yourself that you want to become even if you don't feel ready. It's about having the courage to say "I am a leader" or "I am an artist" or "I am an activist" even when you feel like an imposter.

After Sheryl gave me permission to walk away from Moms Demand Action, part of my renewed commitment to move forward with my fire was to give myself the external title of founder. Until then, I'd been referring to myself as a volunteer, or an accidental activist, or a mom from the Midwest. Calling myself founder felt wrong at first. I wasn't some twentysomething from Silicon Valley wearing a hoodie and jeans. I worried that people would challenge me or accuse me of overblowing my credentials. But I knew I needed to claim my new identity in order to grow my fire and to send a signal to volunteers, to the movement, and to the world—and maybe to myself, too—that I was a leader. I began dressing differently, putting a blazer on over my Moms Demand Action T-shirt. I noticed that other leaders, especially lawmakers, treated me with newfound respect, as if my new title conferred a sense of ownership and authority.

Building your confidence can be as simple as telling your boss you want to learn some new skills, or telling your husband you want to go to couples therapy, or admitting to yourself that you want to work on making more friends. It could be signing up for that genealogy class, or blocking time out on your calendar to practice a new language, or putting a down payment on the trip you've been wanting to take. What's important is claiming the title or identity you want in order to grow both your confidence and your potential.

Say It Out Loud

Sharing your ideas, goals, and desires publicly is an incredibly important way to grow your fire. When you tell someone about what you're working toward, it increases your accountability, which makes you more likely to follow through. In addition, you're creating a positive form of peer pressure that will help push you to keep going. Dr. Herminia Ibarra, a scholar in organizational behavior, refers to this concept as "self-reflecting out loud." When we tell our wants to others, we're better able to clarify our thinking, evolve our thoughts, and enlist others to help us. When you take an internal belief and make it an external declaration, you move closer to becoming that thing.

Amanda Haas says she knew her entire life that she wanted to own her own business related to her love of cooking, but she put her desires on hold for decades to raise her family and support her spouse. After divorcing and walking away from her career, she sat down and wrote a twelve-point manifesto about what her life would look like if she stopped prioritizing what other people wanted her to do. One of her points? "If you want something in life, you have to say it out loud." Then she posted her manifesto on social media. Suddenly, Amanda says publishers and entrepreneurs and investors—almost all of them women—came out of the woodwork to help her find a way to become an entrepreneur. Since then, Amanda has authored four cookbooks, launched an online cooking school, and built a brick-and-mortar cooking school in San Francisco. "What I've learned is that you've got to say the thing freaking out loud!" Amanda says. "And when you do, it's just 'Boom!' It happens. I'm proof of what happens when women say, 'This is what I want from this lifetime.'"

FAN THE FLAMES

Take on a new identity

Add your new identity to your bio online. It can be aspirational or something you already are but haven't yet had the courage to share. After you've done that, can you find the audacity to post about it? You might share something you've recently done in connection with this fire or invite your friends to an upcoming event or gathering related to your fire. Try it the next time you introduce yourself; call yourself something you've never had the nerve to say out loud: "I'm an athlete." Or "I'm a writer." Or "I'm a leader."

Visualize Your Success

Visualization is a mental technique that taps into your brain's ability to react to imagined scenarios as if they are real. Research shows that it can boost motivation, confidence, planning, and resilience—key factors in growing your fire. When you imagine the steps you need to take to grow your fire and then visualize what it will feel like when you do, you're "practicing" success, and that will motivate you to follow through.

When Tina Maat was in her late fifties, she was let go from a decades-long career as an executive chief of staff. She didn't know exactly what she wanted to do next, but she knew she wanted to study astrology, a passion she hadn't had time to explore before. To help Tina visualize the ways she could grow her fire and possibly turn her interest in astrology into a career, she started writing her intentions down on sticky notes, which she put in her pocket and carried with her to keep her fire top of mind. Tina believes that practice helped her create her Etsy store, which sells intention cards similar to the sticky notes she kept in her pocket. "I've noticed that the things I give awareness and attention to—even seemingly small—consistently move from my consciousness into my conversations," Tina says. "And every time I touched one of those notes in my pocket, it reminded me of what I wanted."

Say Yes (Even If It Scares You)

The thing about living on fire is that if you're doing it right, it can feel a lot like fear. Yes, there are many times when it's important or even imperative to say no to things in your life. As we discussed earlier, women are taught to say yes to additional jobs and roles, which only leads to more overburdening to-dos. But saying yes out of obligation is not the same as saying yes to something just outside your comfort zone—something that scares you in a good way and makes you feel exhilarated or brave. Repeatedly saying no to new things out of fear means you'll miss out on important opportunities that could give you a boost of confidence and lead you in directions you never imagined for yourself.

Becca DeFelice, the executive director of Emerge Texas, said her whole life's path has been the result of saying yes to things that scare her. Becca started out as a Moms Demand Action volunteer after her daughter endured a lockdown drill at school. When the organization's Texas chapter was in need of a leader, she said yes again. And when women she met through volunteering encouraged her to run for office, she said yes to that, too. "Growth, to me, is the conscious decision not to say no to leadership opportunities," Becca says. "I look for the need, I am willing to do what I can to fill that need to the best of my ability. That's how I ended up with this life: saying yes a lot."

RADIATE POSITIVITY

Staying positive while trying to sustain your fire will require you to maintain faith in yourself and in your fire, even in the face of failure. It's an act of courage and resilience to know and believe that those failures aren't a referendum on your skills, talents, or worth, they are simply an opportunity to learn and grow. These failures are an unavoidable part of your firestarter journey. In that way, every failure is in fact a success. You can think of failure as an important spark that flies off your fire to help ignite new ventures and new strengths within yourself.

Carol Fricke fell in love with creative writing courses in high school. She planned on becoming an English teacher, but her love for sports overshadowed this plan, and she ended up working as a health and physical education teacher at a high school in Pennsylvania for thirty-five years. After retiring, she began training service dogs, and she was so impressed with the organization that raised and trained these remarkable animals that she got the idea to write a love story based around this process. During her spare time, Carol began plotting out her story—at first, she wasn't sure if she was writing a short story or a novel, but she felt herself come alive every time she picked up her new project. "When I first sat down to write, I just stared blankly at my computer screen. I had no idea how to even start," Carol says. "But I allowed myself the time to do research and practice and just stare into space and think. Slowly but surely, I found my own unique writing voice."

Once Carol finished her manuscript, she decided to try to get her story published. She was determined not to self-publish, believing she and her story deserved to be purchased and promoted by professionals. Over the next decade, Carol continued to send her manuscript to publishers, and even after she was rejected 227 times, she says she never considered stopping. "The first twenty rejections I received were stunning and humbling, but after that I was able to shrug them off," she says. "I knew I was the only one who could and would advocate for myself. I had to believe in my story, even if no one else did." Finally, just after Carol turned seventy, the 228th publisher she sent her manuscript to bought her book, *Detours: A Novel About the Resiliency of the Human Spirit.*

Cultivate a Growth Mindset

Dr. Carol Dweck, a psychologist and Stanford University professor who studies human motivation and coined the term "growth mindset," says that your mindset determines whether you're more likely to lean into challenges and push yourself outside your comfort zone.[1] People in a growth mindset learn to see failure as an opportunity to learn and grow, which helps stave off the fear that can come with change. The opposite of a growth mindset is a fixed mindset, which makes you more likely to shy away from challenges in life or avoid risk due to a fear of failure. Either mindset can affect all aspects of your life, from learning a new skill to finding a new hobby to making a change in your life. You aren't born with one mindset or the other; in order to grow your fire, it's important to pay attention to which mindset you're in and try to shift it away from fixed and toward growth.

Jen Louden, a bestselling author and writing teacher, almost gave up her dream of writing because she was stuck in what she refers to as her own fixed mindset, which she attributes to growing up with several undiagnosed learning disabilities, including dyslexia. Jen moved to Los Angeles and managed to find an agent to represent her as a screenwriter, but she struggled to quiet the voice inside her telling her she wasn't smart or talented enough to grow her fire, so she quit. But her desire to write didn't go away. Eventually, Jen realized she could combine the issues her fixed mindset was causing her with her writing aspirations. That commitment to growing her fire resulted in a bestselling self-help book, *The Woman's Comfort Book: A Self-Nurturing Guide for Restoring Balance in Your Life*, the first popular book about self-care. "I figured out how to change my mindset by digging into my longing, not just to know how to take care of myself, but really how to really love and accept myself," Jen says. "It turns out other people wanted to learn that, too."

A fixed mindset is something Jen still struggles with, even though she's written nine popular self-help books. That includes several abandoned attempts to move out of nonfiction into fiction by writing her first novel. After submitting a first draft to her agent and getting negative feedback about her main character, she gave up and went back to writing what she knew. "It was too hard. It wasn't going the way I thought it should," Jen says. "The fixed mindset wanted to be instantly amazing at trying something new." Because she felt her first draft was not amazing (none are!), Jen put out her fiction fire . . . for a bit. When she got back into a growth mindset, she picked it back up. Now, as a book coach, Jen teaches other women writers how to grow their fires. "The fixed mindset says, 'This is all you've got, and if you can't do something, it's something wrong with you innately and permanently,'" Jen says. "But the growth mindset says, 'Ah, no, you can always grow and learn.'"

Reframe Failure as Progress

Be willing to fail but also to view failure as an opportunity to learn, grow, and try again. Too many women fear failure and see it as an end instead of a beginning of a different way forward. When I started Moms Demand Action, I knew our organization would fail—a lot. After all, we were taking on one of the most powerful special interests in the world. I knew failing would make our volunteers feel demoralized and that, over time, they would leave the organization unless we came up with a way to view those inevitable failures as a step toward winning the next time. And that's how I came up with the phrase "losing forward." Instead of looking at a failure as a total loss, we'd look at it as valuable feedback that would teach us how to proceed and come closer, if not win, the next time. When we lost a battle against a bad bill in a statehouse, we'd recap all the ways we won. Maybe the chapter grew in size because other women heard about our work and became volunteers, or maybe we established new, meaningful relationships with lawmakers. Ultimately, a willingness to fail is also a willingness to take risks, and together, those experiences—even if they're intimidating—help you grow.

LIGHT THE MATCH

Were your losses actually wins?

In your firestarter journal, reflect on a recent failure. Can you find three ways this failure actually benefited or helped you?

Remember Your Why

You don't need to know your exact end point before beginning—in fact, you probably won't see how all the dots connect until you look back at that fire years later—but knowing *why* you want to do something will go a long way toward motivating you. Return to your fire triangle: What are the values, abilities, and desires that motivate you, and will this fire bring those elements into alignment? Return to these motivations regularly and find a way to keep them in your mind's eye so you don't lose track of the desired outcome.

Rennae Stubbs, a former championship tennis player who retired and now works as a television commentator, tells me that anytime she reaches a fork in the road with her fire—elevating women in sports—she looks at the one-word tattoo on her arm that reads "Passion." Rennae got the tattoo so that she would always be reminded of her why: "At some point, all things start to seem uninteresting, or like a drain, or maybe just a little bit too much, and it's easy to get sidetracked. My tattoo brings me back to home base: Passion is why I keep going."

Be Willing to Wander

Because women haven't been encouraged to acknowledge and nurture their spark, the path to growing their fire is often uncharted territory. Maybe along the way, you'll decide you've gone down the wrong path and you want to start all over again at the beginning. Maybe you'll have to take steps backward and sideways before moving forward and then repeat the process all over again. Maybe you'll realize that growth isn't always about adding things to your life but subtracting them. But if you know that spurts of growth are almost always followed by setbacks, you might be less likely to give up because you think you're lost or not gaining ground. Because there's something beautiful about breaking new ground with every step, even if they're not always straightforward.

Stephanie Ruhle, business analyst and television anchor, often reminds herself that her fire isn't linear—in part because she is blazing a new path. Growing up, her mother never worked outside the home, and none of her friends' mothers worked either. As a result, Stephanie worries that she and other women in her generation hold themselves back from going after what they want because they don't have examples of other women to follow. The answer, Stephanie thinks, is giving yourself grace while you wander through your own path. "It's so much easier for men to see all these different paths forward because they've got countless forefathers they can look to who took those paths for generations," Stephanie says. "But, for me, never knowing what's going to come next in my career made me realize my best chance of being successful and fulfilled is being present in the moment. Even if I don't know what's going to happen tomorrow."

LIGHT THE MATCH

The next stage of your fire

In your firestarter journal, write a page or more about what you imagine it will feel like when you reach the next stage of your fire. Name each of the steps it will take to get there and how it will feel when you get there. If you can't imagine or don't know the steps, can you reach out to and/or research someone who might?

FIND YOUR PEOPLE

Even though you don't need anyone's permission to grow your fire, you will need their support. It is difficult, if not impossible, to grow your fire on your own. This is especially true because to begin to grow your fire is to make yourself vulnerable. You are sharing the important pieces of your insides—your values, desires, dreams, and talents—with the outside world. Add to that the understandably daunting challenge of chasing a desire that will likely lead you down an unmarked trail and it is no surprise that most firestarters feel overwhelmed at some point along the journey of building their fire. It is a scary thing that can only be made less scary through the support and guidance of friends.

Friends are a crucial tool for grounding us in our deeper desires. When you feel overwhelmed by an individual fire, friends can help you return to your higher perspective. The friends who support you and your fire may be different than the friends you play pickleball with or the friends you turn to for parenting advice. This support network is made of people who understand what it is you are trying to achieve. Maybe they have even achieved it themselves. These are the people you can turn to in high-pressure moments. They will help ground you and ensure that you are making an intentional decision, not a rash one, just like Sheryl did for me.

In addition to friendship (a benefit of living on fire we'll cover later), having a network allows you to tap into their expertise for advice and support that can help you overcome obstacles and accomplish your goals. Your support system can also provide you with emotional, psychological, and physical assistance when needed. Actively seeking help, accepting it, and nurturing your bonds with those who encourage and uplift you is a powerful strategy for growth. Those meaningful relationships not only bolster your capacity to try new things and handle the challenges that come your way; they also validate the direction and purpose of your fire. Ny Whitaker, a small-business owner and community organizer who was born and raised in East Harlem, says the support from her community was key to growing one of her most significant fires: helping get a charter school off the ground in her city.

Ny had a lot of passion, but she was short on time. Ny says she quickly realized there was no way she had time to travel back and forth from work, as well as volunteer meetings, and manage to pick her son up from school on time. If she could create a system where parents could partner for shared pickups, she'd have more hours in her day to get petition signatures or meet with policymakers. During the next meeting with parents, Ny asked if anyone else was struggling with pickup and childcare coverage. "Organizing is all about support—creating it and then tapping into it. So I said, 'I'm either coming late every day, or I'm picking my kid up late, and I need help,' and that was a game changer," Ny says. "Because then I asked, 'Does anyone else have that issue?' Almost all the hands shot up in the room." She had the courage to say she couldn't do this on her own, which is not something we're always taught.

But the new support system Ny created didn't end when they divvied up their drop-off and pickup schedule. They became a stronger, more connected community when they realized they could

lean on one another. Ny says their support was incredibly important when things got tough, including contentious city council meetings that lasted for hours on end as opposition grew over the funding
and expansion of the charter school movement in her city. "One
meeting about whether our charter school would get authorized
lasted over twelve hours," Ny says. "Our opponents thought that they
could wait us out. But this small little group of us, Black and brown
parents who wanted access to a better education and future for their
children, stayed. Our feet hurt and we were tired. Our kids were
hungry and sleeping on chairs, but we told each other, 'Keep going.'"

Eventually, when the Success Academy Charter School opened,
Ny made sure the support system she built was part of the school's
DNA. Now called a Parent Council, the network provided support
for families for everything from how to oversee and translate their
kids' homework, to assistance for families who speak English as a
second language, to helping families and teachers in need with food,
housing, and clothing at both their charter school and the traditional public school that shared their building. "I encourage women
to say, 'I have greatness and a fire in me, and I want to share it with
the world, but I'm going to need some assistance,'" Ny says. "Because
every time I've raised my voice, I find another woman in the movement who is willing to help teach you or lend money to your cause or
introduce you to someone who can be a connection and help you on
your journey. Whether you're talking about motherhood, woman-
hood, or sisterhood, support is our superpower."

When you're in a moment of overwhelm, think about what you
need. Do you need someone to listen? Are you looking for guidance?
Or do you need someone who can lend a helping hand? Once you
figure out what you're looking for, consider the people you know who

might best suit those roles. It might be a friend, teacher, mentor, or even a mental health professional. Different problems call for different solutions, so it's important to know what kind of support you need as you begin to build the safety net that will encourage you to step out of your comfort zone and take risks. Support tends to fall into three major categories: emotional, educational, and tangible. When you can identify what specific type of support you need and ask for it, you dramatically increase your chances of getting the help you actually want.

Emotional Support

This is the support you get from people who will listen to your ideas and concerns, validate your feelings, and provide you with the encouragement you need to keep growing your fire. They won't necessarily offer assistance or solve your problems; but they'll let you know that they care. If you're stressed, sad, lonely, or overwhelmed, they'll give you a supportive hug to help you through a tough moment and prevent you from turning your back on your fire. Examples of emotional support include giving words of comfort and reassurance, being physically present, and checking in on you to show they care. This is the support provided by motivational cheerleaders who rally around you when you need a boost of confidence or encouragement. These supporters are there to point out your strengths and remind you of your intrinsic value through affirmations and compliments. Life coaches and many therapists offer this type of support to let their clients know that they believe in them, which often helps the clients believe in themselves more.

After Lana Gruell's twenty-year-old daughter Cashleigh died

by suicide, she didn't know where to turn. Desperate for an outlet for her grief, Lana created a grief journal on TikTok. Lana, a mortgage broker who lives in Las Vegas, had never engaged on social media, but suddenly, she was amassing tens of thousands of followers from all over the world. Lana has now expanded her community of grievers to other platforms, which has given her the community she was missing when her daughter died. "Having the ability to open my computer and genuinely connect with other grieving mothers has helped me more than even therapy," Lana says.

A follower who connected with Cashleigh's story and struggled with suicidal thoughts of their own sent Lana a direct message suggesting they work together offline to help prevent suicide. This was the support Lana needed to keep growing her fire. Cashleigh had attempted suicide twice before she died, and Lana had struggled to find the therapy Cashleigh needed. Because of the support Lana received from so many empathetic strangers online, she's now the executive director of the Cashleigh Foundation, a nonprofit organization that partners with mental health services to offer free telehealth therapy to youth across the United States. "The grief is not going to go away. I'll never not cry about Cashleigh," Lana says. "But the virtual sorority I'm now part of reminds me daily that if they can live through their loss, I can live through mine."

Educational Support

These are the people who understand your fire because they've built a similar fire themselves. This support provides the feedback you need when making decisions or changes. These trusted mentors have grown their own fires and have wisdom to share about their own experience, including how to take your next steps or pitfalls you should try to avoid. Educational support can help you feel less anxious when you're dealing with an intractable problem and help you make better decisions. Examples of educational support include instructions and resources based on supporters' lived experiences to help you problem-solve and come up with solutions.

When Jo Ella Hoye, a Moms Demand Action chapter leader in Kansas, was elected as a state representative, the first thing she did was seek out the support of other women lawmakers to help her learn the ropes. This group of women, whom she calls her "sunflower sisters," helped Jo Ella navigate a male-run legislature by becoming her allies and teaching her what they knew, a process Jo Ella refers to as a "transfer of wisdom." One suggestion the women gave Jo Ella early on was to remember that there is no such thing as a "permanent enemy" in politics; that she should always be open to making amends. That advice was particularly helpful after Jo Ella was booed by a male colleague who disagreed with a point she was making on the floor. Afterward, one of the sunflower sisters told Jo Ella who the man was. In an attempt to avoid making enemies, Jo Ella negotiated an agreement with the man to discuss their issues one-on-one instead of on the floor going forward. "Having this network of women to teach and guide helped make me an effective lawmaker," Jo Ella says. "I'm so grateful I never felt like I had to figure it all out by myself."

Tangible Support

These are the supporters who are willing to take on some of your responsibilities so you can focus on growing your fire. That could include lending you their car so you can attend a class or investing in your idea, or making occasional meals for your family, helping with childcare or running errands to give you back some time.

In the early days of Moms Demand Action, the Facebook page I'd created was swarmed by online trolls who seemed to have endless amounts of time to leave comments that were either cruel, misogynistic, or menacing. At first, I would delete every single one of those comments and then block the trolls who left them, something that started taking hours every day. After a few weeks of doing this, I realized there would be no way to get this fledgling organization off the ground if most of my time was spent blocking and tackling online trolls instead of managing the day-to-day operations. Just when I started to worry that I wouldn't be able to get out from under this responsibility, a volunteer sent me a direct message and said, "I see your page is overrun by trolls. I'm disabled and I'm at home all day. Do you want me to manage your page for you?" That volunteer ended up doing that thankless but incredibly important task for years, making our Facebook page a safe space. Her support also gave me back the precious hours I needed to focus on fundraising, organizing, and getting our mission out into the world.

LIGHT THE MATCH

What support do you need?

In your firestarter journal, answer the questions from the beginning of this section to identify the kinds of support you need in order to grow your fire. Do you need someone to listen? Are you looking for guidance? Or do you need someone who can lend a helping hand? As you write, think about the kinds of support you might also need in the future when your fire is fully formed.

FAN THE FLAMES

Practice asking for help

Like any new skill, when you start asking for help it's best to start small. Think of a few things in your life that it would be nice to have some help with—not situations where you feel overwhelmed or desperate for assistance. Maybe you could use help organizing your family's holiday party this year or you'd like an extra opinion on a presentation at work. Then write out a request you feel comfortable with and set a date for when you'll make that request to the person you think would be most willing to offer you support.

Navigating the messy middle of your journey will be one of the most challenging but also rewarding by-products of living on fire. It's where the heat of your desire meets the reality of hard work and unforeseen challenges. It will challenge your values, stretch your abilities, and test your burning desires. It's a period when doubts and frustrations can cause you to question whether you have the strength to keep going. I'm here to tell you that you do. When you feel the inevitable sense of anxiety that too much is happening all at once, remember that this is where you grow. You have the tools to sustain your fire; all you have to do is utilize them.

11

Bonfire

After my marriage ended, I knew my life would change, but I was surprised by how many of my relationships ended when friends or family couldn't understand or accept my decision to divorce. To make it through that period, I had to develop an entirely new network of support. These were friends who understood not just who I was when we met, but where I wanted to go. They respected and supported the life I was building for myself. Their support, which I relied on to make it through the messy middle of my divorce, was my first taste of being a part of a bonfire.

As you live authentically in your fire and build a support system, you'll also grow a bonfire of like-minded women living on fire—a bonfire of women who understand you better, feel closer, and are more trusted than some of the previous relationships in your life. Unlike your firestarter team, which is made up of people who can offer you a variety of support and who may or may not share the passion for your fire, the women you build a bonfire with share the desires, values, and commitment you pour into your fire. The friendships you find through your fire are authentic; when you're living on fire, you're showing up as your true self, not as someone other people want you to be.

Before starting Moms Demand Action, I'd spent my career rising through the ranks of mostly male-dominated companies and fields, and those jobs required me to be my most assertive and aggressive self. I held my ground in meetings, refusing to let men interrupt me or steal my ideas. I wore power suits and pearls. I perfected resting bitch face before it was even a thing. This was a world that was driven by all the things your fire is not: purpose, happiness, and achievement. The work I did was about results, not process. And it was that energy that I led with when I started Moms Demand Action: direct, determined, and even a little dogmatic. That masculine energy definitely helped me get Moms Demand Action off the ground, but it also came at a cost. There are times when I wonder what Moms Demand Action's growth might have looked like if I'd been able to show up as a softer version of myself and still trust that I would be taken seriously. Instead, when people told me I wasn't capable, qualified, or ready to start an organization, I refused to listen and threw sharp elbows at anyone who stood in my way. But then, when I found myself surrounded by compassionate, selfless volunteers and gun violence survivors who served the organization out of the goodness of their hearts, it softened me. I realized leadership wasn't just about strength; it was about the ability to be vulnerable. It wasn't about making people do something because they had to, but because they wanted to. In this new environment, I quickly realized I would have to strip away all the armor I'd acquired and lead with not just authority, but authenticity.

Over time, I learned to be vulnerable about what I was struggling with professionally and personally, which let others see me as a human, not just the impenetrable force trying to take down the gun industry. I made it a practice to express my gratitude—not just for volunteers' time and talents, but for being allowed to lead them. In turn, volunteers gave me their support and friendship. When one of my kids was diagnosed with an eating disorder during the pandemic and all the in-patient facilities I'd called were full, a volunteer helped find my kid a spot in a facility in Denver. After that, I got on the phone with every volunteer struggling with the same issue in their family and told them what I'd learned. When one of my kids graduated, a volunteer helped them get a job. I wrote endless recommendation letters for other volunteers and their kids. Everywhere I went during my travels, volunteers gave me little gifts and cards to thank me for my leadership. I made weekly calls thanking volunteers for their service. This reciprocal dance became an emotional connection that fueled our collective bonfire for years—we all felt seen, heard, understood, and valued. It's one of the most healing things I've ever experienced, and it broke me open.

One of the first women who became part of my bonfire was Lucy McBath. Lucy and I connected just months after her son, Jordan, was shot to death at a gas station by a white man who said her teen's car radio was too loud. Because Lucy grew up with parents who were civil rights activists, Lucy's instinct shortly after Jordan was murdered was to become an advocate to help protect other people from experiencing the same pain she and her family were feeling. Lucy and I connected on a different level than I had ever connected with any friend in my former, pre-divorce life. Lucy and I were warriors together—I would build Moms Demand Action, and as a survivor and spokeswoman, she would bring people in. I was inspired by her determination to honor her son's legacy by working to protect perfect strangers, and she was grateful that I had dedicated my life to the cause. It was Lucy who counseled me on the importance of creating an organization that prioritized diversity—in our volunteers, leaders, and policies—so that our organization was equitable and sustainable.

Over the years, Lucy became a beacon and a friend to me and so many other volunteers and women through Moms Demand Action, especially other mothers who were survivors. It was those women who convinced her to run for Congress after the mass school shooting in Parkland, Florida. Lucy was so devastated by the tragedy that she felt called to run against the congressional incumbent who represented her district in Georgia. It was a longshot campaign—Lucy was running for a seat held by Republicans for more than thirty years in a conservative district, and she was running on the issue of gun safety. But women rallied around Lucy to support her campaign and to get out the vote; in November, despite the odds, she won her race. "Women have always supported me, driven me, prayed over me, and then they lifted me into office," Lucy says.

Working shoulder to shoulder with Lucy to build Moms Demand Action and helping her create a community of women who are both fellow activists and friends taught me that women can accomplish so much more when we come together. This is why your bonfire represents the peak of your fire's growth: It takes your individual impact and multiplies it until there is a network of like-minded women working alongside one another toward a shared cause.

Women's team sports are a perfect example of a bonfire. Devereaux Peters, a shy and reserved introvert, started playing basketball in grade school because it helped her make friends. By the time she was in high school, Devereaux was one of the most valuable players on her team, and she was drafted by Notre Dame. But once she was away from home, Devereaux started struggling with severe homesickness and depression. Her coaches and teammates rallied around her and convinced her to stay. By the end of her college career, Devereaux was a team leader, and even though she wasn't a top scorer, she was a top WNBA draft pick after graduating. Coaches recognized that her ability to support and uplift other women on her team would also help their teams. "Fans think points are the most important thing about a player, but that wasn't my role. I was perfectly capable of scoring a lot of points if I needed to, but I didn't need to," Devereaux says. "My role was doing whatever it took to fit in well with the team and help us work as a unit."

Devereaux still returns to Notre Dame regularly to visit the coaching team and to counsel other members of the women's basketball team. She tells students about her struggle to acclimate at college and encourages players to stick it out during challenging times by leaning on one another. Even though Devereaux no longer plays basketball, the warmth of the friendships from the bonfire she built continues to light her up and inspires the work she's taken on since leaving the court. "I tell the new generation of players that most of my friends are women I met through basketball, especially college basketball," Devereaux says. "It's difficult to be a woman in basketball—people think they know who you are or have opinions about who you should be—but when women stick together, they're stronger. Not just on the court, but in real life, too."

Your bonfire will survive long after you put out an individual fire. Unlike other relationships in your life, which might be built on the role you play in someone's life, such as a wife, mom, daughter, neighbor, or coworker, bonfire friendships are built on the person you want to become. The value of your relationship with your bonfire friend is not measured by how many drop-offs you can do in a week or where you make reservations for dinner. These relationships are about showing up and supporting your friends in the pursuit of shared values. They are about your willingness to go deep and be vulnerable about your path toward growth. They are about wanting to share and celebrate each win and success with other women who recognize the triumphant battle it took to get there. Because of these, bonfire friendships are some of the most flexible yet durable relationships firestarters have. You can call these friends every few months and feel like you are picking up right where you left off.

Brooke Baldwin realized she didn't yet have a team of women like this in her corner when she was covering the 2017 Women's March for CNN as an anchor. Brooke was moved to tears by the communities of women she was interviewing all over the country—women who were coming together in their communities to bond over their shared anger over the outcome of the presidential election. "I had a moment where I realized I didn't have my own huddle to show up at a protest with," Brooke says. "The Women's March made me realize that friendships were something I wanted and needed to start prioritizing."

Brooke began writing her book, *Huddle: How Women Unlock Their Collective Power*, to understand better how women create bonds—through sports, politics, and everyday friendships—and she set out on a journey to build her own bonfire. The women Brooke befriended served as a crucial support system when she decided to leave her job at CNN after thirteen years. Two of those friends even flew out to be by her side at the studio in New York City when she said her last goodbyes on air. Politics and media were not the things these friends valued about Brooke. They cherished her heart and desire to dream big, and they supported her as she put out her fire at CNN and embarked on a new journey.

With more space to reimagine her life, Brooke got divorced, moved to Los Angeles, and landed a new role as the host of a Netflix game show called *The Trust*. Not everyone was excited about Brooke's momentous life changes, but the support from the friendships she'd been investing in emboldened her to be the bravest version of herself. "For the first time, I had the space to determine who was willing to stand by me no matter what, and those are the people who are now my chosen family—women who want my light to shine even brighter," Brooke says. "I had to burn down so many things in my life and let go of people who no longer served me in order to enter this new phase—to birth this person I believe I was always meant to be."

Brooke's journey has had its ups and downs, but her huddle is always there, encouraging her to keep moving forward. "I've spent many days in tears, and it would have been very easy to fall back into what was comfortable in my past life," Brooke says. "Every time I've felt alone, isolated, or unsure, the women in my life have shown up, allowed me to be vulnerable, held me accountable, and given me unconditional support. That abundance mentality helps us unlock the power in one another."

That power often comes from sharing information, but because women who come together to exert their influence and authority threaten societal systems, when women connect and build commu-

nity, they're accused of "gossiping." In the 1500s, actual proclama-
tions prevented women from meeting to "babble and talk,"[1] their
husbands were ordered to keep their wives in their homes, away
from other women. This is precisely why bonfires are integral to
living on fire; they enable women to defy societal values by helping
them reclaim what *they value*.

Melissa Wiley, a children's book author, lived in Queens when
she had her first child in the mid-1990s. Melissa had always planned
to nurse her baby, but when she delivered, she found that her daughter's doctors—mostly men—were unsupportive of her decision.
Like many women, Melissa was reluctant to push back, so when she
struggled with breastfeeding, she bypassed the medical community and called a La Leche League hotline, an organization that specializes in peer-to-peer breastfeeding information and support, for
help. It was there that Melissa found a supportive community of
like-minded women. "It finally felt like, 'Oh, there are other people
like me; I'm not such an outlier,'" Melissa says. "The information
and support I got from these women emboldened me and encouraged me to start standing up for myself."

Melissa enrolled in La Leche's training program to become a
leader, but then her daughter, who was just twenty-one months old,
was diagnosed with leukemia and required urgent chemotherapy in
order to live. Melissa moved into the hospital to care for her daughter. She was determined to continue nursing, something that provided her daughter with comfort and familiarity. Again, Melissa
met resistance from doctors, some of whom made snide comments
about the fact that she hadn't yet weaned her daughter. Then, before
surgery to put a chemotherapy port in her daughter's chest, a doctor
told Melissa she would have to stop breastfeeding eight hours be-

fore the surgery because breast milk was considered a dairy product. Melissa, who knew that breast milk was actually a clear liquid because of her La Leche training, pushed back with data. After a consultation among the medical staff, hospital policy was changed to treat breast milk as a clear liquid, so all babies could nurse until three hours before surgery.

For the nine months Melissa lived at the hospital with her daughter, the women in her La Leche League were the ones who showed up week after week to give her whatever she needed, from meals to tampons to bathroom breaks. "Those women and their support kept me eating, kept me afloat, just emotionally," Melissa says.

And after Melissa and her daughter were finally allowed to go home, the hospital announced that it would start to encourage and make it easier for breastfeeding mothers to continue nursing throughout their child's cancer treatment.

As you nurture your fire and foster authentic connections, you'll cultivate a powerful support system of women living on fire. This bonfire of friendship and mutual empowerment will illuminate your path, offering strength, understanding, and shared purpose. Embrace this journey, knowing that your collective fire will burn brighter and sustain you through every challenge and triumph.

HOW TO BUILD A BONFIRE

Women keep each other's secrets, boost each other's confidence, and serve as coconspirators in their adventures. They teach one another, share information that leads to personal growth and learning, and provide a sense of belonging that is both empowering and inspiring. If you've never had a collective before, don't panic—it wasn't until I was over forty that I started to build my own bonfire. For decades, I told myself I was too introverted, too shy, and too busy to do all the things it would take to make and keep friends. But then, through Moms Demand Action, I found my people—women who were smart, compassionate, engaged, and hopeful. And in each of the three states I lived in while leading Moms Demand Action, my volunteerism led me to communities of women who became my support system. Here are some ways to create your own bonfire.

Find Your People

When Rebecca Bauer-Kahan, the lawyer turned California legislator, decided to run for office, one of her mentors—a woman who had served as the mayor of a California city—warned her that people would let her down, and friends she thought would stand by her would decide they couldn't handle her decision to change course in her life. The mentor was right. Several of Rebecca's friends weren't excited about her decision to run for office, and her closest friend disappeared without giving her a reason. But even though their values no longer aligned, new supporters and friends stepped up to support Rebecca. This new community of supporters rallied around her, with one offering to pick her children up from preschool every afternoon, another who was a professional party planner helping to plan house parties, and others who knocked on doors and made phone calls to get out the vote. In the end, the support of these new friends who, like Rebecca, valued putting more women in office made the difference between victory and defeat—Rebecca ended up beating her incumbent opponent by just a few thousand votes. "I said, 'This is the space I want to take in the world,' and if some people can't be here for that journey with me, I give them that grace," Rebecca says. "But the women and friends who respect me and love me for who I am showed up in ways I never imagined. They believed in me, they had my back, and, in the end, they were who helped get me elected."

This powerful transformation can happen when women combine their collective fires. If, like Rebecca, your fire involves large groups of women, it might be easy to join an existing bonfire. But if your fire is something more isolated, like working from home or caretaking, you'll likely need to make a conscientious effort to create your own. But in either scenario, be prepared to take a risk and make yourself vulnerable, like a kid in the middle school cafeteria looking for a place to plant their tray. If you are middle-aged, that can feel daunting, but it doesn't need to be. When relationships are based on shared values, it's easier to make that first small bid for connection.

Bare Your Soul

Being vulnerable is crucial in developing close friendships. But if you're facing a barrier or stuck in a trap, you might find it difficult to let other women genuinely get to know you and share a sense of emotional intimacy. When you meet people you want to connect with, commit to being brave enough to open up to them. Being vulnerable allows your friends to support you and show that they care, and it builds trust, closeness, and connection, strengthening your collective resolve.

After Michelle Sinnott left her job as a firefighter to stay home with her newborn, she realized she wasn't just lonely but depressed. She spent months isolated in her home and found it difficult to make herself do the things she'd enjoyed before giving birth, like mountain biking or meeting with friends. Eventually, Michelle was diagnosed with postpartum depression, but it took a long time for her to feel like herself again, and she felt self-conscious about telling other women what she'd gone through. But after a national shooting tragedy, Michelle started to worry about whether her son would be safe when he eventually started school. She Googled to find an organization she could support and saw there was an upcoming Moms Demand Action meeting near her home. She showed up, and not only did she meet other women who shared her values, she was able to share her story and connect to other women who had struggled with the same depression she was emerging from. "After feeling dead inside for several years, I was suddenly in the company of all these women I could be myself around, and I started to feel alive again," says Michelle, who went on to serve as a local group leader. "Being with all these incredible women after I hadn't been connecting with people provided the spark of reconnection I needed."

The bonfire you build won't just make you feel less alone; it can also make you feel more secure. It was that bonfire of feminine energy that drew in Dr. Annie Andrews, a pediatrician who felt stymied by all the men in her work world who were either training or managing her. In fact, at the time Annie decided to volunteer with Moms Demand Action, she had never once had a woman as a supervisor. "I wouldn't have felt confident enough to walk into that first Moms Demand Action meeting if it hadn't been a space full of women," Annie says. "I didn't know anything about gun violence, community organizing, or activism at all. But I walked in and immediately felt comfortable and welcomed. And then the relationships that I built with the women who were in that room, that very first meeting, those are friendships I still have today."

That's especially important if you're taking on a task together that's difficult or controversial, like standing up to armed extremists or a bully on your local school board. Stephanie Lundy, a Texas Moms Demand Action volunteer who signed up the day after the Sandy Hook School shooting, says she and her fellow volunteers could never have withstood the threats and intimidation they received if it hadn't been for the camaraderie among the women who started as strangers and became friends and teammates. Their strength came from being honest with one another about their fears. After they shared that they were all frightened by the possibility of being confronted, they could look one another in the eyes with bravery and say, "Okay, but we're still going to do this anyway."

"We never knew what we were walking into in those early days; there were all these guys with guns, and they'd go online and threaten to kill us if we showed up at our statehouse," says Stephanie, who met the women she now calls her best friends through her volunteerism. "Our ability to laugh at these men and with each other was such a crucial way to overcome our fears and to connect. Our vulnerability with one another helped us create a safe space— not just to protect us from the gun extremists, but also to be our most essential selves."

What Stephanie and her friends understood is that the best and fastest way to build your bonfire is to go deep and commit fully to being vulnerable. Opening up can feel uncomfortable and scary, but it shows others that you're committed and provides others with the opportunity to reciprocate your vulnerability, which is the secret sauce to deepening friendships over time.

A simple but powerful way to build trust with your friends is to be honest about your struggles. We're all always struggling with something—it's a common thread that connects us all as humans. You don't have to share the most intimate details of your life, but you do have to share something personal. Practice starting a sentence with "I'm struggling with" and then fill in the blank—my job, my anxiety, or my marriage. You'll be surprised by the response; when you're vulnerable, people will be more willing to share their struggles with you, too, bringing you closer.

Grow Together

Many friendships end when circumstances change. You move neighborhoods, change jobs, or start dating someone new, and the friends you thought were forever fall out of your life with surprising speed. Other friends might see change as the inevitable beginning of the end, but bonfire friends will rally around you to support you through this new stage. You may even find that as your friends continue on to new ventures beyond the first fire that brought you together, your bond deepens as you can offer one another support through new challenges and celebrate hard-earned wins.

When Jennifer Herrera decided to move on from Moms Demand Action, the fire that brought her to her new collective, she found this to be true. Her bonfire friends weren't upset that she was trying new things without them; they were thrilled for her. Ironically, Jennifer wasn't looking for friends when she joined Moms Demand Action. She was the mom of two young boys and was pregnant with her third when the Sandy Hook School shooting happened. Jennifer was so distraught that she felt if she didn't get involved in gun safety activism, she'd feel complicit the next time she heard about a shooting. Jennifer went online and found an event she could attend near her Virginia home—that was the beginning of a six-year journey that would lead her to become the Virginia Moms Demand Action chapter leader.

Jennifer grew the chapter to thousands of women across the state, helped flip the makeup of the state legislature to a gun sense majority, and laid the foundation for nearly a dozen new gun safety laws to be passed due to those electoral wins. In the process, Jennifer found her people—doers and changemakers like her who wanted to save lives. "It was magical to be surrounded by women who had completely different life experiences, women of different ages, different backgrounds, different ethnicities, and yet we all shared the same heart," Jennifer says. "It was like living inside that GIF of the women who are endlessly lifting each other up by the hand."

After leading the Virginia Moms Demand Action chapter for five years, Jennifer knew it was time to make more space in her life to pursue other causes that were important to her. She handed over the leadership baton and took the skills she'd learned to a new job: She joined the leadership team at the National Women's History Museum, a museum dedicated to celebrating women's diverse contributions to society and helping women and girls see their potential and power. When she left Moms Demand Action, one of Jennifer's biggest fears was that she would lose her activist community. But even as she evolved, Jennifer has maintained and grown her friendships with other volunteers, many of whom have also moved on to other organizations. When the museum hosts events, Virginia volunteers show up to support Jennifer. "No matter what I'm doing or where I live, I will forever be a part of a community of women pushing for change."

When you unite with other like-minded women, the collective power of your fires will grow exponentially. And the beauty of a bonfire is that you can carry its warmth and light with you from fire to fire. Like Jennifer embarking on her new mission at the National Women's History Museum or Brooke deciding to leave CNN, fire-starters know that when they're transitioning from one fire to the next, their bonfire is the place to go to for support. The relationships you build through bonfires are a vital source of energy to tap into as you put out one fire and begin another.

FAN THE FLAMES

Add someone to your bonfire

The next time you encounter someone who you think would make a good addition to your bonfire, plant the friendship seed with a simple but genuine compliment. Try for something deeper than "I like those shoes." You might say, "I like your style," or "What you said in our meeting really resonated with me." If you are feeling extra bold, you can add, "I think we could be friends." It might feel too vulnerable, but the reality is most people *are* looking for friends, and hearing that someone sees them as a potential pal is an effective way not only to make your intentions clear but to help open up to other people.

PART
FOUR

Protecting
Your Fire

My phone vibrated on my nightstand, waking me from a sound sleep. I assumed it was one of my kids calling with a middle-of-the-night crisis, which could have included everything from lost keys to acute heartburn. I picked up my phone and held it to my face; it was three in the morning, and the call was coming from a private number. I silenced the phone and laid it back on the nightstand. Minutes later, it vibrated again. I turned it off and went back to sleep. The next morning, I woke up to dozens of voicemails from men menacingly daring me to just try to come for their guns, as well as hundreds of emails and direct messages with subject headers like "Come and take it, commie bitch" and "Hands off my guns, hag."

This harassment at all hours of the day had been going on non-stop since I'd started Moms Demand Action a few months earlier. I'd received letters mailed to my home, complete with cutouts from magazines to spell out threats to my life. My email had been hacked;

my Facebook photos were downloaded and distributed publicly; my phone number and home address were shared online; my children's social media accounts were hacked, and the names of their schools were shared online. But the harassment wasn't just coming from behind a computer screen—extremists, almost always men, had started showing up at Moms Demand Action events with loaded rifles to intimidate us. The underlying message: Stop talking about guns, or we'll harm you or someone you love.

Later that day, after seeing a man idling near my driveway in a pickup truck and taking photos of my house with his phone, I decided it was time to call the police. When the officer arrived, the truck was gone, but I hoped he would give me some advice on how to handle the threats and maybe even agree to have his patrol keep a closer eye on my home. After I explained that I'd recently started a national organization to fight for stronger gun laws in the wake of a mass school shooting, the Indiana officer, who'd been taking notes during our discussion, looked up at me with a stern expression and said, "Well, ma'am, this is what you get when you mess with the Second Amendment."

I was incredulous; it was one thing to get trolled by gun extremists; it was quite another to be reprimanded by an officer of the law—someone whose job would have been made safer by stronger gun laws. Later that evening, I called my dad to tell him about what had happened, hoping he'd give me some guidance. When I was growing up, my dad had always been the person I'd turned to when I needed help solving a problem. But after I detailed all the threats I'd been getting and recounted my discussion with the officer, he was silent. I thought maybe he was pausing to consider some suggestions, but instead, he said, "Do you think all this danger is worth it? Because these threats are just going to continue as long as you're trying to take people's guns away."

That comment stunned me even more than my conversation earlier in the day with the police officer. Not just because my father didn't seem to understand the mission of Moms Demand Action— we wanted to restore the responsibilities that go along with gun rights, not strip them away—but because I was being admonished by someone who actually knew me. Someone I'd assumed would support me and be on my side. But his words of warning made me wonder if he was right. Was it possible I was on the wrong track? So many strangers seemed to think so, and now the person who'd taught me right from wrong did, too. And what would our disagreement mean for our relationship if I continued with my activism?

After an exhausting day, I didn't have the energy to argue with my father about the technicalities of the Second Amendment, so we agreed to disagree and hung up. But something I'd sensed since starting Moms Demand Action was now startlingly clear: Blowback—not just from strangers but from friends and family, too—was the price I'd have to pay for being a woman with a strong opinion about guns. And the only way to keep my fire going was to learn how to endure it.

12

Preparing for Blowback

I tell you this story not to scare you, but to assure you that you, too, can stand in the flames and emerge even stronger. While the blowback I've experienced is extreme and unique to my fire, any woman who becomes a firestarter will have to endure the unfair and inevitable consequences women are expected to pay for living audaciously. Just like the blowback that happens when fire is trapped in closed spaces—the flames suddenly and explosively reverse course and go in an unexpected direction—as your fire grows, you will inevitably feel your fire turn on you, and the heat from its repercussions may burn.

That criticism will kick into high gear when you're growing your fire. As you fan the flames, the sparks your fire throws off will make people pay attention. Suddenly, you'll start to feel and appear bigger and brighter, and people will see you in a different light. Some people will wonder with awe, "Who is this person behaving so boldly?" But others, alarmed by your audaciousness, will see you and think, "How dare she?" That is when you'll start to feel the heat. Friends might ask you if you feel bad that you missed your child's recital because you had a meeting for your new business. Coworkers might complain that you aren't the team player you used to be now that you are setting harder boundaries around work. Neighbors might comment on how lucky you are that your husband is willing to take on childcare while you focus on your personal goals. This pattern will play out in your neighborhood, in your workplaces, with your friends, and even in the pickup line at your kids' school.

Up until this point, you've worked hard to find the courage to build your fire. You've grown comfortable with your own discomfort and battled your bad beliefs, and so far, your efforts may have only yielded positive results. But eventually, someone will decide that your fire has grown too large and too bright, and the blowback will begin. Unlike the setbacks we strategized against earlier in the book, which are more likely to be circumstantial, blowback feels personal. It may feel like anger, rejection, disrespect, or ridicule. More likely than not, it will come in the form of criticism. This type of negativity poses a real threat to your ability to live on fire because it doesn't just attack the success of a single fire; it strikes you at the heart of who you are. It can make you doubt your belief in and commitment to your desires, values, and abilities, and embolden that negative inner voice you've worked so hard to silence. But remember, all the criticism you get when you dare to live on fire is predictable. None of it is personal.

If your fire is strong enough to create blowback, chances are you've learned to silence, or at the very least manage, your inner critic—but all of us have our breaking points. For many women, that point comes when outsiders affirm society's bad beliefs about women on fire. They retreat into the familiar, though painful, space of their negative inner voice, listening to its commands, which, more often than not, leads to unwarranted self-sabotage.

Every time Michelle Sinnott starts a fire and begins to grow it, she backs away and lets it die out. The first time it happened, Michelle was chasing her childhood dream of becoming a professional dancer. After years of dedicating all her free time to practicing and competing, Michelle finally became one of the top dancers in her troupe. However, she began ruminating about her competitors, imagining she wasn't as talented as they were. Within a year, Michelle dropped out of dance and felt such shame for quitting that she struggled with self-harm and disordered eating.

Years later, after Michelle recovered, a friend took her mountain biking, and she rediscovered her love of physical movement. Michelle became obsessed with mountain bike racing and was so good at it that she joined a team in Japan and was able to support herself financially through sponsorships. But just as Michelle's fire grew, the pressures and fears associated with competition crept in again. As Michelle started to doubt whether she was good enough to race professionally, she found herself slowing down whenever she was neck and neck with a competitor during a race. She was throwing her races to avoid the shame she would feel if she tried her hardest and still lost.

Michelle quit racing to become a firefighter, but once again, she convinced herself she wasn't strong enough—mentally or physically— to compete with an almost all-male brigade. After several incidents that made Michelle feel like she didn't measure up to the rest of the firefighters, she decided to leave the force. Now, when Michelle looks back at this pattern that has played out nearly every time she's pursued a passion, she realizes she internalized societal penalties and punishments for being a woman in fields that aggrandize men. "Consciously, I realize I have a deep-seated fear that I'm unworthy," Michelle says. "But when I'm trying to make something happen in my life, it's difficult to recognize in real time that I'm falling into a trap of my own making."

Michelle has internalized the blowback she's experienced over a lifetime, and now, every time she gets close to getting what she wants, she relapses into feelings of unworthiness. For Michelle (and many women), being on the receiving end of criticism is so painful that in order to prevent it—along with the pain it engenders—she becomes her own worst critic instead.

THE EMOTIONS THAT THREATEN TO EXTINGUISH YOUR FIRE

Women put their fires out prematurely to avoid what I call "extinguishers." These are the emotions, typically ungirded by guilt or shame, that lie dormant until you begin to push the boundaries that constrain you and, when triggered, threaten to keep you small. These extinguisher emotions are caused by how we handle blowback. Some women can wave off judgment like an annoying fly, but other women will hear that external criticism as an affirmation of their negative inner voice. This inner voice holds on to all the shoulds you worked so hard to overcome when you decided to build your fire. It wants you to stay small and safe, to keep the status quo. Tara Mohr, a coach and an expert on women's leadership, says that even when women are fighting to live outside the system, they're still programmed to try to appease it: "As human beings we are hardwired to stay in our emotional safety zones, which means that, consciously and unconsciously, we try to avoid doing anything that will result in criticism, failure, or feelings of guilt and shame. And because powerful women are often so harshly criticized or shamed, women can end up not using their voices and gifts because of fears of what may come in response."

Guilt

For many women, guilt is an ever-present emotion. It is a self-conscious and even chronic feeling that one should bear remorse or responsibility for letting themselves or others down by not living up to some unrealistic or unattainable expectation. Just like the shoulds we discussed earlier, guilt is often associated with obligations: Guilt is the blame we feel for not meeting expectations that we *should* do something we don't want to or can't do. Guilt is especially easy to trigger when growing your fire because it will require you to make choices that prioritize your fire over other things in your life. That might mean missing a kid's soccer game, ignoring after-hours emails, or asking a sibling to check on an aging parent so you can focus on your fire.

Those choices are hard for women to make. Women carry immense responsibilities, which can feel devastating when left unfulfilled. Guilt is a zero-sum game that women can never win. You feel guilty about working too much but also about working too little. You fear you're coming up short as a parent, but also that you're too involved. You've taken on too much but don't feel you deserve to take time for yourself. This guilt can be paralyzing, making it difficult to assert your needs or follow your desires without simultaneously feeling like a failure.

During one election cycle, I tried to balance my obligations with traveling across the country to help get out the vote with my other roles as colleague, partner, and parent. At the same time, one of my children in college had been hospitalized with an eating disorder. I was working to coordinate their care, from finding the right inpatient facility to navigating their insurance coverage. I didn't want to walk away from my activism, but I also needed to care for my kid. I battled feelings of guilt and shame every day. Was I a good mom? What did my ex-husband think when I asked him to take our child to the doctor for the tenth time? Would my child resent me for trying to parent and work simultaneously? But I felt like I was doing an okay-ish job of keeping all the balls in the air until I was invited on the podcast of a famous male political pundit.

During our pre-interview off air, I mentioned that my kid was struggling and that I was exhausted from being on the road. It was, I thought, informal banter about our lives before we went on air. But during the interview, the podcast host brought this conversation up on air and asked me if I thought my child's eating disorder might be the result of my being such a busy mom. At first, I was gobsmacked, and then I was mortified. His words tapped into the inner voice that had been telling me I was a bad, selfish, uncaring mother for continuing to work. All the worst things I thought about myself were true. At least, that's how it felt because someone else seemed to believe them, too. I tried to give a straightforward, unemotional answer, but after the interview, I lay on the floor of my hotel room and stared at the ceiling for an hour. It was the closest I'd ever come to walking away from my fire—not because my child wanted me to, but because a question that felt like veiled criticism triggered my guilt and shame.

So many women have told me that the blowback of mom guilt—the implication that a child will somehow suffer if their mother pursues her own fulfillment—is what most often prevents them from growing their fire. But mom guilt is man-made; it's society's way of reining in women's desires. Caitlyn Collins, an assistant professor of sociology at Washington University in St. Louis and author of *Making Motherhood Work: How Women Manage Careers and Caregiving*, says guilt encourages women to blame themselves for falling short instead of questioning why they don't have more support from the system. "Guilt serves as a regulatory mechanism because it benefits men, employers, and the government for women to feel guilty. It pushes women to strive harder every day to do more, to take on more, to fulfill more needs, to meet more of their children's desires," she says.

I know this firsthand because my children are now all adults, and when I ask them if they ever felt neglected or ignored when they were younger and I was working and traveling, the answer is unequivocally "no." In fact, they're proud of my accomplishments, and they say my independence forced both their dad and stepdad to step up, which gave them more equal time with all three of their parents. Your kids won't remember the occasional soccer game or school field trip you miss; they'll remember all the times you did show up, and they'll be proud you created a meaningful life, which will encourage them to do the same. As psychologist Dr. Aliza Pressman told me, "When you do the thing that lights you up, it gives your child a role model on how to find meaning in your life, and that entire meaning cannot come only from our kids," she says. "If you're suffering because you're not giving yourself the time, space, and energy to make sure you're fulfilled, you're not doing anyone any favors. We have to show our kids they can be free to live their lives happily, that our happiness does not rest on them, and that we can find meaning both as mothers and separate from motherhood."

Shame

Over time, when women hold themselves to a high standard and still feel or are told they're coming up short, their consistent feelings of guilt can turn into shame. Guilt tells you that you did a bad thing, but shame is more insidious—it tells you that you're a failing person at your core. And because women are more likely to interpret criticism as information about themselves as opposed to the opinions of the person giving them feedback, blowback can start false shame spirals in our heads. The more you become convinced you cannot meet your or others' expectations, the more you believe you're unworthy. That's why the guilt and shame ignited by criticism are such profound and powerful extinguishers—they make you feel you are fundamentally flawed, striking you in the heart of who you are.

Sandra Cisneros, the daughter of Mexican immigrants, says she "grew up wanting to be a woman without shame," but the shame she felt about her impoverished childhood and wanting to be a poet, and her guilt from an affair she'd had with a professor in college, prevented her from exploring her gifts. It wasn't until she was willing to examine those feelings that she was able to unlock her creativity and claim her identity as a writer. Specifically, Sandra says it was her internationally bestselling book, *The House on Mango Street,* a story about a Chicana growing up in a poor and patriarchal community, that helped her "compost" her guilt and shame: "I found a way to uncensor myself by taking my emotions and transforming them," she says.

Sandra, who never married or had children, now writes poems about the freedom that comes from shedding light on the shame associated with being a woman. "I want women not to be ashamed of their bodies. I want them not to be ashamed of getting older," Sandra says. "It's been a lifelong process to realize that what I thought were the disasters of my life, things I felt ashamed about, actually helped me claim my creative gifts," Sandra says. "For so long, shame made me feel like an imposter. But now, at age sixty-nine, I can finally say I am a poet who writes stories. I am free to claim my gift."

LIGHT THE MATCH

Nurture yourself through tough emotions

In your firestarter journal, reflect on how your body signals guilt and shame to you. Do you feel heavy? Tired? Maybe even a little bit queasy? Make note of what or who in your life triggers these feelings for you. Think of five ways you can nurture yourself before and after you have to interact with this person or thing that stirs up these emotions in you.

Even when you know that what you're doing is right and good for you and your family, the pressure and discomfort you will feel when you seek out what you burn for will sometimes seem unbearable. This is the double bind of fucks-giving for women. To start and grow your fire, to fight for your fire, you must care deeply about your values, well-being, and desires. You need to be determined to make a difference in your life or the lives of others. You need to give all the fucks.

But to protect your fire, you have to learn to give zero fucks. You must stop caring what others want from you or what they think about you. It's a pathological predicament that requires women to be both hard and soft in the world. Depending on the situation, they must be both impenetrable and vulnerable. I have no remedy for this dilemma because I know firsthand that it is almost impossible to strike an acceptable or tolerable balance of fucks. All I can tell you is that to survive the blowback you will inevitably face, you must get comfortable with making other people uncomfortable.

Olivia Julianna, the Texas activist who found her fire when she started taking on lawmakers online when she was just a teen, felt the blowback of standing up for herself right away. Online hate and harassment, especially toward women in marginalized identity groups, can be especially virulent in digital spaces, and Olivia says the comments section of her posts was full of the worst things you can imagine ever saying to another person. But instead of just blocking and reporting her tormentors, Olivia decided to take their hate on directly by calling them out and elevating their attacks for others to see. Because the haters knew that Olivia was going to stick up for herself and even exploit their hate for her benefit (including raising gobs of money for her favorite issues), the hate slowed down . . . somewhat.

"So often, women are told to 'sit down' and 'be quiet and be nice and respectable,' but there comes a time when you have to fight fire with fire," says Olivia. But the blowback she has experienced hasn't just happened online. She's lost relationships with childhood friends and even family members who oppose Olivia's support for issues like abortion rights. "I came to understand that when you're speaking truth to power and fighting for what you believe in, not everyone will support you."

Pushing back against cultural conditioning isn't easy, and learning to withstand blowback is a discipline that will take practice and time. With every fire you start, you strengthen your fortitude to stand firm in your beliefs—even when the world would rather you stay quiet. This doesn't mean you have to fight with people in the comments of your social media posts. It means you can face confrontations and discomfort without abandoning yourself. Ultimately, the degree to which you can grow your fire is directly proportional to the amount of blowback you're willing and able to withstand.

13

The Traps Extinguishers Create

I t's inevitable that you will be criticized and that those criticisms will trigger feelings of guilt and shame, but falling into the traps those emotions lure you into is avoidable. The goal of this section is not to teach you to avoid the challenges or the hurt that will be a part of your firestarter journey—in fact, avoiding pain is often how we get trapped in patterns of self-sabotaging behavior in the first place. Instead, I want you to practice challenging the inner voice that tells you to avoid blowback at all costs—to keep growing your fire, even when it feels like it would be so much easier to walk away. And the first step in that process is learning what to expect; if you know what is ahead, you can prepare yourself to withstand it.

In this chapter, I outline the emotions that blowback gins up, the traps those emotions set, the reasons it's so easy to fall into them, and how you can stay out (or get out) of them. By learning how to avoid these emotional traps, you'll realize that almost every solution for bypassing them requires you to accept the discomfort that comes from saying no, standing by a boundary, or unapologetically going after what you want. Certainly, that's no easy task, but it's better than the pain of betraying your values, your needs, your wants, and—ultimately—yourself. Here are the self-sabotaging traps firestarters will need to navigate as they grow their fire.

SELF-JUDGMENT

Because women are judged so harshly by society, they learn early on to continually scan the horizon for any blowback caused by their perceived shortcomings, hoping and praying they'll be able to identify and correct them before anyone else notices. This is the first stage of the trap of self-judgment. Your negative inner voice tells you that you can prevent unwanted criticism and ward off rejection if you constantly compare yourself to others and measure your worth by external validation. But to protect yourself from the judgments of others, you end up judging yourself more harshly than anyone else would.

Every thought becomes a menacing warning of how you're falling short. "I would like to spend more time with my kids" becomes "I'm neglecting my kids and failing as a mother." "I would like to broaden my friend circle" becomes "I'm unlikable and will always be lonely." "I want to learn a new skill" becomes "I'm not as accomplished as my colleagues, and I'm falling behind." That's why self-judgment threatens your fire: The negative talk track in your mind will immobilize, not motivate, you by generating so much trepidation about every move you make that it becomes a self-perpetuating cycle. You judge your actions, which leads to inaction, which leads to self-judgment, until you become stuck and suffer as a result. "When you're believing what your inner critic tells you, you could easily convince yourself, 'Oh, actually, I can't go do that next thing because I'm not qualified. As you live with that thought for another five or twenty years, the inner critic ends up directing your choices. But it's our values and aspirations—not the inner critic—that we want steering the course of our lives," Tara Mohr says.

Amanda Haas had a dream of becoming a cookbook author for years, but she put those desires on hold, not because she wanted to, but because her negative inner voice told her that if she went to work, even part time, it would make her a bad wife and mother. Amanda says this belief came from her upbringing. She even judged her friends for choosing to work and putting their kids in day-care. But when she and her husband experienced financial bumps, Amanda was forced to return to the workforce. She quickly realized that the self-judgment she'd consented to was wrong and limiting. "I look back and wonder why I listened to that voice for so long, a voice instilled in me by the patriarchy," Amanda says. "The second I stepped into the building on my first day at my new job, I was like, 'Oh, this is what it feels like when you stop listening to society and allow yourself to be ignited by something other than being a mom.' Judging myself and others had boxed me in for so long."

Assessing whether you've fallen into the trap of self-judgment means noticing if you're constantly comparing yourself to others. If you stay in your safe space, you'll likely police others to stay in that safe space, too. Buddhists call this the comparing mind: You determine your social and personal worth based on how your inner voice tells you you stack up against others. This leads to negative self-talk that erodes your confidence and stops you from growing your fire because you assume you will fail before you even start. That dialogue might sound like "I'd like to start my own business, but I don't have enough experience for people to take me seriously." Or "I've always wanted to write a book, but who actually would want to read it?" Instead of judging yourself for wanting to create a meaningful life, remember that you don't have to follow the rules of a system that prevents you from feeling at ease. With practice, it's possible to learn to differentiate between the voice of self-judgment and the voice of truth. The next time you receive criticism that activates your negative inner voice, pause and review this list of strategies.

Assess the Criticism

Just because someone judges you doesn't mean you have to believe it. Women are criticized so often and about so many things that you begin to assume it's warranted. But usually, criticism says more about the criticizer than the person being criticized. Try to view criticism as feedback you're free to take or discard based on who delivers it. If someone cares for you and has your best interests at heart, you can choose to consider their input (knowing it isn't gospel). But if someone doesn't know or value you, be aware that their feedback isn't grounded in truth.

Julia Boorstin says that during her journalism career, she's been told that she's pushy in her interviews or aggressive in her reporting—despite operating just like her male counterparts. However, while writing her book, *When Women Lead: What They Achieve, Why They Succeed, and How We Can Learn from Them*, she discovered research that found that women are more likely to get feedback on their style than on their substance. "Now that I know that, I see the negative feedback I get has nothing to do with me," Julia says. "I'm just not acting in a way that aligns with someone else's stereotype. It's incredibly liberating to realize that because I'm a woman, some people expect me to be warm and nurturing, and that's not my problem; it's theirs."

Interrupt Negative Thoughts

You already know that negative thoughts will come; make it a practice to pay attention to them, acknowledge them, and then let them go. The only way to break the cycle of self-judgment is by making a conscious effort to interrupt and analyze those thoughts instead of believing them and buying into the blowback. You can use many tools to prevent you from latching on to bad beliefs about yourself, including mindfulness meditation—the practice of anchoring your attention on your breath and staying present without getting lost in judgments, stories, or assumptions.

Sharon Salzberg, a Buddhist practitioner and renowned meditation teacher, started meditating decades ago to help heal her judgmental thoughts. She grew up in a chaotic household, including a parent who died when she was young. That experience led Sharon to seek out ways to alleviate her suffering, including her feelings of guilt and shame. "Meditation is a training in resiliency," Sharon says. "Instead of focusing on the constant self-judgment that can make you feel demoralized and exhausted and leads nowhere, you focus on returning to your breath again and again with a full heart. Eventually, you can lessen the negative thoughts."

Replace Judgment with Compassion

It's possible to replace your negative talk track with a gentler and more loving mantra that encourages you to view your perceived flaws or failures as temporary thoughts or behaviors. You don't have to do years of meditation training or enroll in a spiritual study to get in touch with your higher self; you can tap into your inner well of self-compassion just by pausing to talk to yourself lovingly. And the more you show yourself compassion, the more your inner voice will reflect those affirmations.

Dr. Kristin Neff, a self-compassion researcher and author, says learning to show yourself kindness can help women become more accepting of themselves *and* strengthen their resolve to grow their fire. "Women aren't supposed to rock the boat, so part of self-compassion is learning to be okay with embodying fierceness," Dr. Neff says. "Self-compassion teaches you that you're worthy of doing whatever lights your fire, and that's incredibly freeing."

FAN THE FLAMES

Get feedback from your firestarter team

The feeling of not being enough is likely one of the most pervasive forms of suffering in our culture. Reach out to your firestarter team to set up a time to reflect on your feelings of self-judgment and ask them to share a story about a time they wrestled with similar feelings.

MARTYRDOM

In our culture, there is a pervasive belief that a woman cannot do well unless she's doing good, unless she sacrifices her own needs and desires for the good of others at all times. So once you begin to grow your fire, it's logical that you might be tempted to try to prove that you can do both: be a good girl *and* live on fire. But when you position your fire as a service to others at your own expense, you fall into a trap that can put out your fire: Because you feel ashamed of focusing on yourself, you begin making sacrifices that can be harmful, including forgoing self-care or glorifying your suffering to get validation. You convince yourself that to grow your fire, you have to make sacrifices that not only ward off blowback but also engender recognition, attention, and validation. Martyrdom can serve as a security blanket, a way to protect you from judgment and criticism. Because, after all, who will criticize a victim or a hero?

I know this trap firsthand because I fell into it as soon as I started Moms Demand Action by deciding early on that I wouldn't take any pay for my work. That was partly because we hadn't raised enough money to pay anyone but also because it felt noble to be seen as a volunteer rather than a lobbyist. For eleven years, I stuck with that narrative: I was a good girl whose credentials couldn't be doubted because I was volunteering out of the goodness of my good-girl heart. And, to be honest, it did help me avoid the blowback that would have come with being a woman leader who wasn't just high-profile but also highly paid. And because my husband was able to financially support my family, not taking pay helped assuage the guilt and shame I felt about my privilege.

This is what's called a "passion tax." Women who are passion- ate about their work are exploited by employers who convince them to work longer hours, take on additional tasks outside their role, or accept lower or no pay because "the work is its own reward." Just because you are paid for work you love doesn't mean you are com- modifying your passions in a way that betrays your fire. Even if— especially if—you are passionate about your work, you deserve to be paid for your labor.

During my tenure as Moms Demand Action's leader, I sacri- ficed hundreds of thousands of dollars in income while working longer hours than I ever had in my previous career. All the while, the organization's male leaders were paid handsomely for doing less. And yes, I can see now that I was taken advantage of by the leaders who never offered to pay me, even after the job became all- consuming, but I also allowed myself to be taken advantage of. I built a cross, fastened myself to it, and then looked down at every- one else and proclaimed, "Look at me, a good girl whose intentions are pure. How dare you criticize anything I do when it's for free?" I told myself my sacrifices were for others when, in reality, they were in my own self-interest. The problem with not taking pay for all my hard work wasn't just that it was harmful to me; it was a poor stan- dard and a bad example for other women who deserve to be com- pensated for their labor. I deserved to be compensated for my labor.

Society celebrates the selflessness of women leaders and how much they're willing to sacrifice. As a result, martyrdom is the only kind of hero status that's acceptable for women to attain, and we don't talk about it because it might make us look like narcissists (another common criticism of women) or, worse, our status might get taken away from us. Sarah Hartley, the woman who started a magazine focused on women's issues, says it wasn't enough that she thought what she was doing was important—she needed everyone else to know how hard she was working and, like me, that she wasn't getting paid. "I posted a lot on social media about how hard it was to run the magazine; that in addition to working at a full-time job and taking care of a newborn, I was up until all hours of the night packaging up magazine issues, designing the next issue and editing essays," Sarah says. "Otherwise, I worried my work would be seen as a silly hobby or something that wasn't valuable and took too much time away from my family."

For the first three years she published her magazine, Sarah repeatedly told her subscribers that every penny her magazine brought in didn't go to her but to keep the magazine afloat. Because it was a goodwill project to share women's stories, Sarah felt it could only be considered authentic and valuable if her work was undervalued. Sarah now realizes she was also trying to avert the criticism she'd seen other women creators get for trying to make a living from their creations. But the magazine eventually folded because she didn't promote herself or her magazine's success, including its impressive number of subscribers. "I'd witnessed the blowback women get when they not only dare to lead but actually make a living from it, and I think a part of me believed that if I was doing this heart and soul work, that meant I shouldn't be making money from it," Sarah says.

To determine whether you've veered into the trap of martyrdom, ask yourself if you're masking your desires and accomplishments with ways to dismiss or diminish yourself and your actions, like claiming that all your actions are fueled by selflessness for fear that you will appear self-interested. That could include staying out of the spotlight or failing to take credit for your successes.

Also, take stock of how your sacrifices make you feel; selfless-ness can make you resent others who aren't martyring themselves, too. Self-sacrificing is often profoundly engrained in women and embedded into our lifestyle, making it difficult to parse out. Still, there are steps you can take to shift your thinking away from self-lessness and toward valuing and caring for yourself.

Stop Being Selfless

Women are told in so many ways—overt and subtle—that if they're not being selfless, they're being selfish. It's right there in the words: loss of self. But selflessness is a trap that requires you to prioritize the wants and needs of others over your own to the extent that you eventually lose sight of yourself and the fire you were growing. But you're not obligated to sacrifice your well-being for others; you have the power to make choices that prioritize yourself.

In her book *Untamed*, Glennon Doyle writes about this trap—how women are so conditioned to martyr themselves, especially as mothers, they learn to live as though "she who disappears the most, loves the most. We have been conditioned to prove our love by slowly ceasing to exist." Glennon goes on, "When women lose themselves, the world loses its way. We do not need more selfless women. What we need right now is more women who have detoxed themselves so completely from the world's expectations that they are full of nothing but themselves. What we need are women who are *full of themselves*. A woman who is full of herself knows and trusts herself enough to say and do what must be done. She lets the rest burn."[1]

Reframe Your Thoughts

One way to diminish your desire to martyr yourself is to replace the negative self-beliefs telling you women should be selfless with more balanced and realistic perspectives. This takes practice and time, but when you can create a pause through reflection, you can use that beat to better understand the beliefs and emotions driving your behavior.

Dr. Jessi Gold, a psychiatrist who specializes in treating burnout, says that noticing these thoughts, many of which are ingrained and subconscious, is the first and essential step to breaking the pattern. "Because women don't have many role models of what leadership looks like, and because we're inclined to want to lead differently than men do, it can turn into a catch-22 where we worry our assertiveness will look like arrogance or narcissism," says Dr. Gold. "But by noticing those thoughts, it's possible to reframe them and to switch from someone who is always sacrificing or selfless or overburdened to someone who is aware of and values their unique contributions."

Remember That You're a Role Model

If you're a mom struggling with putting yourself first, remember that you're setting an example for your children. If you teach them that you don't value your worth or put yourself first, they will learn to do the same. But if you show them by example that everyone benefits when they have meaning in their lives, they'll also treat themselves that way. And you're not just a role model for your family—other women are watching you, too. See your fire as a gift to yourself and others.

Gisele Barreto Fetterman, the mom of two who became a firefighter in her forties, has the same mindset; she believes that when mothers feel guilty, they teach their children to perpetuate self-punishment. "I don't want my children to learn to feel guilty because they're not enough, or they didn't do enough, or they have to be everything to everyone else," she says. "I don't need to be a perfect parent; my love is consistent. I want them to see me pursue my passions, I want them to see me be brave, and I want them to see me support them but also follow my dreams. That is the biggest gift I could give them."

FAN THE FLAMES

Trust the pause

The next time you are asked or offered to take on a responsibility, pause for a moment before responding and ask yourself: Is this something I would choose to do if no one was watching? Let the answer be your guide as to whether or not you take on the responsibility.

PEOPLE-PLEASING

Women are socialized to be more accommodating and nurturing than their male counterparts from a young age. While all humans want to be accepted, women are taught that being amenable is a desirable feminine trait and that assertiveness or aggressiveness is unattractive. As a result, you might bend over backward to do favors you don't want to do, apologize constantly or unnecessarily, and sacrifice yourself when you don't want or need to in order to overcompensate and preempt blowback.

People-pleasing is one of the most pervasive ways women attempt to avoid criticism. If you're a people pleaser, you will find yourself overcompensating by doing whatever is necessary to ensure people—including perfect strangers—aren't put out or put off by the space your fire occupies. You tell yourself that if you're always on your best behavior, if you lack boundaries, sacrifice your wants and well-being, and apologize constantly for mistakes you didn't make, you will be able to protect yourself from the discomfort of making other people uncomfortable.

As Iranian immigrants, Mandana Dayani's family brought their cultural hospitality to Los Angeles. Mandana was raised to always project pleasantness and to downplay any negativity or problems that might make others uncomfortable—a behavior exacerbated by her need to assimilate into a new culture. As she got older, this ingrained performative behavior turned into people-pleasing. Even though she was a lawyer with an enviable track record of accomplishments, Mandana became fearful of taking risks in case she disappointed her family or community. Eventually, Mandana found practicing law so unbearable that she made the agonizing decision to quit her job as a lawyer (agonizing mainly because it would require her to displease her parents). When she sat down with her father to tell him she wanted to do something else in her career, he told her that happiness was not the point of employment. "That conversation made me realize people-pleasing had cost me years of happiness," Mandana says. "But it also woke me up. I had put my fulfillment on hold to please people with a totally different cultural mindset than I had as someone raised in America."

These pleasing behaviors are especially prevalent when fire-starters start to find their stride. Just as they begin to prioritize their fire over the needs of others, they get criticized for shifting their focus. Criticism begins to pour in, and feelings of guilt and shame pop up, along with the discomfort that comes with making changes in your life. You might be caught in the trap of people-pleasing if you believe that protecting yourself by setting and keeping healthy boundaries is selfish or unkind. If you're taking on more and more responsibilities, even though you don't have the capacity or don't want to do so, you may be trying to be all things to all people. But pleasing others at your own expense won't make people appreciate you more; it will make them value your time and contributions less. And by giving all your time and energy to please other people, you take the focus away from growing your own fire. Here's how to start putting yourself first.

Set Boundaries

Boundaries protect your fire by giving you the physical and emotional space to focus on yourself. By communicating your needs and expectations clearly and respectfully, you create boundaries that will protect your time and energy for growing your fire. Make it clear to people what you are willing and able to give them. People-pleasing often involves neglecting personal boundaries, constantly accommodating a friend's needs, and sacrificing personal goals to maintain the friendship. If you only have ten minutes to talk before your sibling calls, tell them as soon as you answer that you only have ten minutes.

After initially pursuing a career in medicine to please her parents, Nazanin Boniadi realized as an actor that people in Hollywood were taking advantage of her tendency to please others. Inspired by the courage of the women activists in Iran who speak up despite the costs and what she calls a moral obligation to protect younger actresses who might be taken advantage of, Nazanin is learning to set healthy boundaries through mentors and therapy. "People imply that you're difficult or even unhireable in Hollywood if you say no or set a boundary around what you will or won't do, but I now realize that that's a form of gaslighting—a way to stop women from using their power," Nazanin says. "I've come to understand the profound strength in standing by my values and confidently voicing when a behavior crosses my boundaries. Staying true to myself, even in uncomfortable moments, empowers me to create healthier, more respectful interactions."

Disconnect from Other People's Opinions

When you focus on pleasing others, you create a disconnect between who you are and who you're pretending to be in the world. Instead of focusing on your own fulfillment, you put your energy toward pleasing others to earn the gold star or accolade. But not only is it exhausting and impossible to please everyone all the time;

eventually, you might start to believe that people are drawn to the persona you've created and that you aren't known for who you truly are.

To differentiate between constructive feedback and unhelpful judgment, Dr. Jessi Gold counsels her patients to consider whose opinion it is and whether that person has relevant experience or is simply projecting their insecurities. Everyone will have opinions about you, both positive and negative," Dr. Gold says. "You can't control what others think of you, but you can gain perspective and control how you feel about or react to that opinion."

Learn to Say No

When you agree to help others at your own expense, you prioritize their wants and needs over your own. While it can be positive to offer kindness, empathy, and support occasionally, it can become dangerous when you do it despite your own needs or never say no when you want to. In fact, one of the most empowering things you can do is to learn to say no to things that don't light you up and honor your fire. Dr. Gold says one way to figure out whether you should say yes or no to any ask is to put together one list of all the things you're willing to say yes to, and a corresponding list of all the things you don't value or want to do—things that are always an automatic no. Putting those yeses and nos on paper serves as a people pleaser's North Star when they're tempted to take on more out of guilt, not passion. "When you make what you are and aren't willing to do nonnegotiables, it takes some of the pressure off what saying no says or what people might think about you," Dr. Gold says. Keep in mind, your list can include off-limits topics or content areas, people you don't want to work with, and boundaries related to your time and emotional energy.

FAN THE FLAMES

Give yourself time

If saying no feels scary, start by practicing saying, "Let me think about it," each time a new opportunity or request comes your way. In doing so, you give yourself more time to evaluate whether you want to actually do what you are being offered *and* time to craft a thoughtful but firm response.

DISAPPEARING

When women are criticized, they often view it as a referendum on their worth or popularity—a testament that they are worthy of being seen. So then, when someone accuses them of falling short, the guilt and shame they feel for being seen as a failure makes them want to run away and hide. Shame involves an uncomfortable sense of exposure that naturally leads to wanting to disappear. When you withdraw, you don't have to deal with your mistake, the people you imagine are judging you, or the shame you feel for failing. It is a temporary bandage on painful emotions, but more often than not, it can lead to totally disengaging from your fire.

Let's return to Becca DeFelice, the Texas woman who ran for office twice and lost. After each of those experiences, she realized that because she'd had the audacity to "fail" in public, she was expected to step off the stage and retire to the comfort of her home, where she could marinate in her embarrassment in peace, and then never attempt to achieve anything of import again in her lifetime. "I've experienced it, but I've also seen it in my work helping women to run for office: Any time a woman steps out in a public way to lead and falls short of their goal, they are shamed into not existing," Becca says. "Because if you're a woman who loses, you're suddenly the embodiment of *every* woman who has ever lost anything; a living, breathing reminder that when women try, sometimes they'll lose."

Consider this imposter syndrome in reverse: Just as there are few examples of other women who are in power or in the spotlight to follow when they succeed, there are also too few examples of how women should behave when they fail. Men fail spectacularly and publicly all the time, but instead of shrinking, they know that they'll be given the grace to try again. From good guys like Beto O'Rourke to bad boys like Elon Musk, men who fail rarely leave the stage after a significant loss. In fact, their failures can serve as a springboard for bigger and better things. For men, failures are temporary setbacks, but for women, missing the mark is an excuse to be discarded.

But that isn't the only reason women are discarded. As women age, they are suddenly invisible in a culture that values the beauty of youth. The blowback can be severe if you insist on taking up space after age forty. Geri Jannarone, a political activist in New Jersey, was raised by a mother who, like many women in America, believed her value was inherently tied to her physical appearance. Geri says that as her mother aged, she became increasingly frustrated with the effects of aging and began slowly disappearing from public life, including cutting back on work and socializing. "My mother was furious about aging, and I watched it devastate her physically, mentally, and emotionally," Geri says. "I told myself I was never going to agonize over aging the way my mother did, but here I am, almost sixty years old, and asking myself if it's time to get off the stage."

Geri's inherited a subconscious belief that she should cater to the male gaze. It wasn't as problematic when she was a young woman working her way up the ranks of New Jersey's political system. Her youth was a skeleton key that unlocked all kinds of opportunities in a world dominated by older white men. But now things are different. During a recent meeting, a former colleague implied that Geri was too old for her position. "I noticed that as I got older, doors closed, and people stopped returning my phone calls," Geri says. "So when someone says I'm too old for my position, it activates that negative inner voice that tells me I should stay out of spaces I used to feel comfortable in."

Geri says it took her years to realize that her concerns about what other people think of her age or looks is rooted in childhood trauma that morphed into a harsh internal critic. She had a breakthrough in both confronting and quieting that voice when she was hired to revise a political training program designed to teach women in her state how to run for office. One of the training modules focused solely on helping women learn how to "dress for success," encouraging women to wear understated jewelry and dress a certain way. Geri immediately cut the module from the curriculum. "I just thought, 'I am not buying into that,'" she says. "I will not continue to buy into one goddamn bit of the entrenched patriarchy that tells me and other women they have to look a certain way."

Geri finally realized that other people's perceptions of her and her abilities only had power over her if she allowed them to. And that instead of withdrawing, she could reframe how she felt about herself. Of course, it's normal to want to escape the blowback—your brain is wired to protect you by telling you to avoid or run away from situations likely to elicit uncomfortable emotions. But this survival instinct isn't always accurately interpreting the threat—just because you feel threatened doesn't mean you have to fall into the trap of automatically removing yourself from harm's way. When you disappear, you validate the inner voice that says you're not worthy and confirm other people's criticism that you should go away in the first place. It may be essential to step back from a situation if you're struggling mentally or physically, but if you're only withdrawing to escape uncomfortable emotions triggered by criticism, it might also be a valuable opportunity to grow your tolerance for feeling uncomfortable and, in turn, grow your fire.

Next time you feel the urge to retreat, review the strategies below for ways to manage the tough emotions and make a game plan for how you'll stay in the arena.

Hold Your Seat

It's only natural after a loss or a failure to want some time to recoup, reassess, and heal before you return to the stage, but a tactical retreat is different from a shameful one. If you start to feel the urge to run and hide in the safety of your bedroom, pause and ask yourself, "Why do I feel this way?" Then, to distance yourself from your thoughts, name the emotion that wants you to disappear, and remember that critical thoughts or words do not define you. Standing your ground even though everything inside you is telling you to run will help you get comfortable with being uncomfortable.

A'shanti Gholar, the president of Emerge America, has endured misogynoir for everything from her braided hair to her clothing to her body. The hate made her want to hide, but she fought against that desire and stood her ground. Along the way she learned that the blowback she gets for being an audacious Black woman is not about her but the person criticizing her. "Criticism about my race or gender is always coming from a place of negativity, and other forms of criticism are often based on envy," A'shanti says.

A'shanti tells the women she trains to run for office to prepare for the blowback coming their way, and uses her own experiences to show them how to keep it from holding them back. "Something I always hear so often from women thinking about running for office is 'I don't want to be criticized,' and I tell them they're going to be criticized no matter what. Unfortunately, people will always talk about you if you're a woman," A'shanti says. "But wouldn't it be better to have them talk about all the ways you're setting the world on fire?"

Keep Showing Up

It is your right to make mistakes; it's a part of being human. Just imagine the knowledge, influence, and networking power we lose when women feel they need to leave the stage. Instead of shrinking, go on offense by continuing to show up. This approach is a type of desensitization. Keep exposing yourself to situations that make you want to disappear until the feeling goes away. Being an on-air news personality for decades has meant *Morning Joe* cohost Mika Brzezinski has been constantly criticized for her looks. That scrutiny, especially as she aged, made her self-conscious and eventually led her to have a chin tuck years ago. She thought her procedure was a private matter until, shortly after the 2016 presidential election, Donald Trump, the newly elected president, tweeted about the procedure in an attempt to shame her. Trump, who disliked her coverage of his campaign, called her "low I.Q. Crazy Mika"[2] and said he had once seen Mika "bleeding badly from a face-lift" during an event at his resort.[3] When a colleague showed her the tweet on his phone, Mika said her reaction was disbelief. "There are a lot of things that loser gets away with, and one of them is cruelty toward women," she says. "But he wasn't going to get away with this."

Mika could have let the president's insults diminish her—make her disappear—but instead, she used them to spur a worldwide conversation about misogyny and how women are shamed for aging. A whole community of women rallied around her, including women leaders in the Republican party who called the president out publicly. Mika had the last word: The president could criticize her face, but she kept showing up and using her voice to speak out against his behavior. "I'm in my late fifties, and even though I thought that the opposite would be true, I'm more comfortable with myself than I've ever been," Mika says. "I spent a lot of time trying to conform, but now I realize my beauty is in my fire."

FAN THE FLAMES

Ask for accountability

When you feel the urge to disappear, tell someone on your firestarter team. This simple act of enlisting a friend to check in is a crucial strategy for accountability.

LIGHT THE MATCH

Prepare to respond to blowback

In your firestarter journal, create a blowback response plan by listing all the shoulds you had to overcome at the start of your fire journey. Do those bad beliefs still threaten your fire now? Highlight the criticisms and the critics that hurt you the most, and then reflect on any traps you may have fallen into in an attempt to avoid blowback. What are the strategies you can use from this chapter to prevent yourself from falling into those traps going forward?

As women, we often find ourselves walking a tightrope, balancing our desires with societal expectations, criticism, and our inner negative voice. But learning to handle blowback is an opportunity to build your resilience and, ultimately, to strengthen your ability to live on fire. The ability to differentiate between constructive feedback and unwarranted criticism rooted in societal biases and prejudices will provide you with clarity that can help lessen the sting from blowback that has absolutely nothing to do with you and everything to do with the person reacting to your fire.

For the first several years of my leadership at Moms Demand Action, I was constantly worried about the blowback that was coming my way every time I made a bold statement on television, or encountered an unsupportive neighbor in the post office, or shared a story about gun violence on Twitter, or agreed to a debate with an opponent. Sure, I'm precocious by nature, but I'm not immune to the societal shoulds I've been taught about how "good" girls and women behave. But, along the way, I decided that as a mother, if I lost my children to gun violence, I had nothing left to lose. I decided I should embody that "zero fucks" philosophy as an activist.

I've learned that I actually love fanning the flames; I now look forward to the blowback I know is coming my way when I say something provocative or unladylike or even just the truth. That's because I know that other people's opinions about me or my stances aren't personal and because I've learned that the path to living on fire is not about avoiding criticism but facing it head-on with courage and conviction. As you navigate your own firestarter journey, try to expect (maybe even look forward) to the blowback. It can be difficult to face the unfair criticisms that are thrown at women who dare to live on fire, but they're also proof that you are on the right path.

14

Burnout

Trying to manage the emotions and exhaustion that come from navigating the gauntlet of extinguishers and traps set for women who dare to live on fire can deplete your energy and lead to burnout. If you constantly judge yourself, those feelings of inadequacy build up and sap your energy and motivation. If you're always sacrificing for others, you will eventually feel the effects of neglecting your own needs. If you can never say no to taking on more tasks and responsibilities, the frustration of overcommitting will take a toll over time. And if you respond to stress by withdrawing again and again, you will eventually feel disconnected from yourself and your spark.

That was what Amanda Doyle realized when she finally decided she had to make space in her life for fun and play. "I realized I wasn't leading my life. I wasn't saying this is how much I want to do here; this is where I want to end. Instead, I say, I'll know I'm done when I pass out. But if I could say to myself, I don't actually have to earn my worth on this planet . . . I would have more play. I would have more humanness." Living in this constant state of burnout and exhaustion that Amanda describes is normal, everyday life for many women, but it shouldn't be.

Burnout, a term used to describe when a fire is extinguished because there is nothing left to burn, is a metaphor for a state of physical and emotional exhaustion, similar to how a fire burns out when it runs out of fuel. There are plenty of books about burnout that explain what it is and how you can avoid or remedy it. What I want us to focus on together is how burnout can prevent women from living fulfilling lives and how you can protect your fire from being extinguished by the inevitable overload of living as a woman in a society that expects you to keep going no matter what.

We often talk about burnout in correlation to a job or career, but it can appear in all areas of your life, from parenting to caretaking to friendships and romantic relationships. Any time you push yourself too hard and for too long, the positive energy you initially felt for an idea or person can be replaced by cynicism, anger, hopelessness, or apathy. This is not the same thing as stress, which is a short-lived sensation tied to a short-term goal that we all feel in bursts on a regular basis. Burnout is typically accompanied by feelings of emptiness, apathy, and hopelessness. Because our culture doesn't allow women the time to take stock of their emotional health, you might not realize you're burned out until your fatigue manifests as physical exhaustion or pain.

In the wake of the 2016 election, the singer MILCK (Connie Lim) found herself growing a giant fire. After she struggled for years to support herself as a singer-songwriter, a song she wrote about her sexual assault and her experiences of being an Asian American woman called "Quiet" became the unofficial anthem of the Women's March. MILCK and her song went viral, and she was immediately signed by a major record label and began working on a new album. It was the kind of success story most artists dream of, but for MILCK, the blowback she was experiencing as part of her success—like limiting comments about being "too different," too political, or not universal enough—triggered an avalanche of emotions, including guilt and shame.

To cope with these uncomfortable feelings, MILCK found herself inhabiting every single trap I previously outlined. Because she underestimated her talent, she thought she needed to overcompensate. Because she felt a responsibility to give back after her song became a social justice anthem, she dedicated all the proceeds she received to charity. Because she wanted to please the team at her label, she allowed them to convince her to make rushed choices. And eventually, because MILCK felt unsure if she was deserving of being in the public eye, she found herself shrinking and wanting to disappear altogether. "No one tells you how to navigate what happens after that first spark of success," MILCK says. "When all those feelings based in fear push on us, it's difficult to know in the moment how to push against expectations or free yourself from the firestorm you're in."

MILCK, who had struggled with disordered eating, suddenly found herself driving in the middle of the night to Jack in the Box, ordering a massive amount of food, and then zoning out at home in front of the television. She began drinking to get through her recording sessions. And, like my own experience with what happens when you tamp down negative energy, MILCK began breaking out in hives and experiencing vertigo. After a few years, MILCK realized her new life was untenable. In order to get back to her original spark, she would need to cull everything that was preventing her from focusing on what was most important: her music. MILCK left her label to make and release music on her own terms. "The burnout wasn't a fast fall to my knees; it was a slow burn," MILCK says. "I felt like I was making mediocre art that didn't inspire me, and I started to see that I was slowly dying by trying to be something for everyone else but me."

Avoiding blowback can cost you valuable energy, the essence of your fire. Add to that the exhaustion from all the roles you're asked to inhabit, from full-time employee or stay-at-home mom to volunteer, friend, partner, and on and on. As the saying goes, you can't pour from an empty cup.

When you look at a calendar that is stacked full of work and family obligations, it's tempting to tell yourself there is no time for you to pursue your fires. You may even feel burned by past experiences when you did try to start a fire in your life, only to end up exhausted and overwhelmed by the effort of living on fire and fulfilling all the roles you play for your family, friends, and coworkers. That was the experience of Anushay Hossain, a women's health advocate. Anushay had always wanted to publish a book about how the healthcare system discriminates against women. Ever since her traumatic experience after giving birth, she'd been building a fire focused on educating other women on how they could advocate for themselves within the healthcare system. After publishing her book, *The Pain Gap: How Sexism and Racism in Healthcare Kill Women*, during the pandemic, she reached a breaking point. Even though she'd wanted to write a book her entire life, the stress of publishing and promoting it while taking care of her sick parents in Bangladesh and her young children at home in Washington, DC, while also dealing with side effects from perimenopause proved to be too much. Anushay noticed that drinking helped her not think about how overwhelmed she was. "After managing everyone else's emotions all day, I drank a bottle of rosé before bed and then passed out," she says. "It started as a way to escape, but then it started to make me feel depressed and anxious."

Anushay went to her doctor after she started having panic attacks that she thought were heart attacks. Her doctor told her that on top of her anxiety, approaching menopause had sent her hormones into a tailspin. That appointment was a wake-up call. Anushay realized she needed to prioritize taking care of herself. "I didn't realize how exhausted I was until that appointment; I just kept going and going. But then, after totally burning and crashing, I knew I needed to stop drinking, get a therapist, get a personal trainer—whatever it took to start feeling better," Anushay says. "I know all these people need me, but first and foremost, I have to take care of myself to take care of them, too."

FIGHTING BURNOUT

Like so many women, the guilt and shame of burnout brought her to the land of "self-care." One type of self-care is called faux self-care, and it won't help you sustain your fire—in fact, it's just one more thing you'll be adding to an already overflowing plate. Faux self-care isn't actually care, but a capitalist solution to the problems created by a capitalist system that ends up benefiting the system more than the person it burns out. After creating pathological levels of anxiety and exhaustion in women, we're told the "solution" to burn-out is spending money we don't have to get back to a baseline of feeling normal. Faux self-care has turned into an entire industry that profits from patching up women's broken bodies, minds, and souls to make sure they stay productive. Unfortunately, faux self-care won't fundamentally change anything. All the bath bombs, essential oils, and meditation apps in the world can't fix your burnout. "Toxic wellness isn't self-care—it's a marketing opportunity," says Dr. Pooja Lakshmin, a psychiatrist specializing in women's mental health and the author of *Real Self-Care: A Transformative Program for Redefining Wellness (Crystals, Cleanses, and Bubble Baths Not Included)*. "Because women and mothers have tremendous economic power, they're told that the solution to their problem is something they can buy."

The other kind of self-care, the kind that will help you nurture and sustain your fire, is what Dr. Lakshmin refers to as "real" self-care. It's the process of learning how to create boundaries that protect you from overwhelm, practicing self-compassion when you feel things slipping through the cracks, returning to your values when you don't know how to allocate your time, and then harnessing all that newfound power to protect your fire. Dr. Lakshmin points to one of her patients who struggled with breastfeeding her baby; she found it physically painful and mentally taxing, and as time went on, it made her resentful toward her baby. After agonizing about what she should do to best take care of herself and her child, she decided to switch her baby from breastfeeding to formula. It was a deeply personal choice, but by permitting herself to set boundaries that aligned with her values, she could spend more time doing things that made her feel good about herself, like going to her moms' support group. "Real self-care is a practice, and it boils down to doing fewer things, being nicer to yourself, figuring out what matters the most in your life, and then continuing to do more of that," Dr. Lakshmin says.

Most of the firestarters I've worked with and interviewed have learned—some the hard way—that self-care protects you from burnout by restoring the energy you need for firestarting. Like Nazanin Boniadi, who only commits to three months of activism at a time so she can recharge in between, or Mallory McMorrow, the Michigan state senator who found herself working during legislative breaks so she started proactively blocking time on her calendar for yoga classes and vacations with her family; or Lisa Ling, who is committed to a regular breath work practice; or Jerri Green, who signed up for a twenty-four-hour sauna and goes whenever she can, including late at night after her kids are asleep; or Jennifer Siebel Newsom, the First Partner of California, who told me she gets together regularly with her friends for something she calls "balming," which is taking time out of their busy lives to nourish their souls through nature, art, and culture. These self-care routines are not about gaining the instant validation a face mask or a manicure can provide. These practices allow firestarters to ground themselves in their bodies and feed their souls. Here are a few practices you can try when you start to feel the burnout take hold.

Rest

The reality is we need a lot more rest than we realize, and more often than not, we only give ourselves rest when we are way past the point of exhaustion. The thing about rest is that unlike many of the faux self-care practices wellness companies try to sell women, it's free. Yes, it can be challenging to find time in your busy schedule, but we can all manage to give ourselves ten to twenty minutes of downtime. When you start to feel like life is too much and you can't keep up, instead of doubling down on your to-do list, take a nap, sit quietly, or go for a walk (and no scrolling!).

Movement

One of the most reliable ways to metabolize stress and anxiety in your body is to get active. That might seem counterintuitive when you feel tired and overwhelmed, but movement is how your body moves out of its stress response. When your body recognizes stress, whether that's a serious threat to your safety or a dauntingly full calendar, your system is flooded with cortisol and adrenaline. For most of human history, stress was a response to immediate physical threats, and our choices were to fight those threats or flee them. But in today's uber-connected world, threats like constant emails from work, texts from friends and family, and never-ending news alerts are far more difficult to escape, leaving our bodies trapped in the stress response. Simply stretching or moving through some yoga poses can help reduce the levels of stress hormones in your body.

Compassion

Burnout is particularly lethal for women because while we're doing one million things for others, we often still feel like we somehow aren't doing enough. These feelings are rooted, as we discussed earlier, in the pernicious emotions of guilt and shame. When you start to feel those negative thoughts bubble up in your mind, take a moment. Pause. Instead of letting those thoughts pick up steam, give yourself a hug—literally. Compassionate touch for twenty seconds can help lower those stress hormones I mentioned above. Remember that you are doing all that you can do and that is more than enough. Talk to yourself like a friend.

The reality is that building and sustaining any fire takes an immense amount of energy. It would be unrealistic to assume that you can add finding your fire to the rest of your normal, everyday life and not expect to encounter some challenges. As you work on growing your fire, remember that your self-care practice needs to be proactive and ongoing if you want to prevent burnout. But once you get to the stage of burnout, and most of us will get there more than once in our lifetimes, take it for what it is: as an undeniable sign that something important in your life is not working, and it's time to identify the underlying causes of your burnout and clear some space to regain a sense of balance and purpose.

FAN THE FLAMES

Conduct an energy audit

If you're feeling burned out, it's important to take stock of all the ways you're expending your energy. Write down everything you do in a week, from leading weekly team meetings at work to helping your kids with their homework after school. Then categorize the different types of energy (physical, emotional, or mental) each activity requires and then label them 1 through 10 to determine how much energy each activity takes. When you review your audit, look for anything that seems to take a significant amount of energy or seems glaringly off balance. Are there places where you can cut back and reserve your energy?

15

Controlled Burn

Creating space to live on fire might seem counterintuitive, but remember, learning to live on fire doesn't mean you need to do more—it might mean you need to do less. There are a lot of things you may be able to cut back on or responsibilities you can shirk for a little while as you focus on your fire, but some things—and some people—might need a stronger course of action. And while few of us have the privilege of being able to quit our jobs, hire a nanny, or move off the grid, we can do something I call a "controlled burn," a way to audit all the demands on your time and decide what to do less of, what to do more of, and what to get rid of altogether.

For centuries, some Indigenous groups have practiced what they call "good fire"—controlled burns that act as medicine to the environment, balancing and restoring the ecosystem and lessening the risk of wildfires. These prescribed burns don't just prevent fires that are out of control; they rejuvenate the forest floor by returning nutrients to the soil and removing debris, which creates new and open space for sunlight. After a controlled burn, new growth, like saplings and seedlings, begins to grow. This principle of fire management is just as true for you as it is for the earth.

Conducting a controlled burn in your life will preserve your energy so you have enough for your fire. That could be as big as ending a relationship, stepping away from a job, or reassessing how you parent, or as small as giving up a volunteer role that's taking too much of your time or changing how you consume Netflix or social media. Controlled burns are practices of self-care that clear the debris in your life and create space for you to unearth the version of yourself that is more authentic to who you truly are, but they are also ways to reform yourself into something more powerful. They are ways to remove things from your life that no longer serve you and, in turn, to protect your energy.

After my epiphany in Dr. Miller's office, I took an inventory of what worked in my life and what didn't. Obviously, my marriage went in the "not working" column, and I wasn't willing to stay in it indefinitely just because I feared the blowback I'd get from the world. Certainly, after I made my decision, lots of people had opinions, and some even suggested that I should feel guilty or ashamed of divorcing, given that I had three small children at the time. I was told in a million different ways by both people I loved and perfect strangers that I was selfish, immoral, and a bad mother. I had a choice about how to react: I could give in to the blowback that told me I should feel guilty or ashamed and stay in a marriage making me physically ill, or I could listen to the inner voice telling me to move on. So, I returned to my journal and, once again, made two lists to help give me clarity about how to proceed. One list included everything in my life—people, places, opportunities—that made me feel alive and supported, and the other included everything that no longer served me. And I did the same again when I started Moms Demand Action.

As you start your own fires, you'll realize there's also a lot of unlearning and even subtracting of what's not working. You might have to disrupt what previously existed in order to create a fresh, open space that allows for new experiences or people to be invited in. Charlotte Clymer knew that coming out as transgender would force her to make major changes in her life. But the former West Point cadet had reached a point where she couldn't pretend anymore, and she knew it was time to be open and honest about a secret she'd kept since childhood. "I'd gotten pretty decent at concealing the fact that I was in agony, but the more that time went on, my tolerance started to dip," Charlotte says. "By the time I finally came out, I was exhausted. It was either kill myself or come out of the closet."

Charlotte shared her story on her award-winning blog *Charlotte's Web Thoughts*, where she writes essays on the intersections of a wide range of topics from her perspective as both a progressive trans woman and Christian military veteran. She knew that writing about who she really was would result in the loss of significant relationships in her life, especially people she'd befriended in the military and at church who might not be able to reconcile who Charlotte had pretended to be with who she really was. And she was right. While many of those close relationships survived—and were even strengthened—some of the people Charlotte thought she was close to never spoke to her again, including her father. "Sadly, it's not an uncommon experience in the queer community, and I knew instinctively that once I came out, my father would disown me," says Charlotte, who re-created her support system with what she refers to as her chosen family. "When given a choice between being suicidal and maintaining a relationship with my father, I chose personal liberation."

Controlled burns can be just as freeing when they are done on a small scale. After MILCK cleared her obligation to her record label, she lost a lot of security, including her income and health insurance, but she regained the ability to hear her voice again. That started with challenging her eating disorder, which told her she should stay small. MILCK began an experiment; she told herself it was okay to gain weight and see how it felt. To withstand the discomfort of the inner and outer voices telling her she'd gotten too big—literally and figuratively. Over time, MILCK grew out of the clothes she'd once worn. As part of her controlled burn, she threw them away and bought clothes that wouldn't restrict her.

FAN THE FLAMES

Conduct a controlled burn audit

Review your time and energy audits to see if your lists include any activities you don't want to do—things you're doing out of obligation or habit. Can you control-burn five things you're doing robotically that will give you some space? Maybe it's the time you spend scrolling through social media, running errands that aren't urgent, binge-watching Netflix, or helicopter parenting. Maybe it's a relationship with a friend who has turned into an energy vampire, someone who feeds on your willingness to listen and care for them, leaving you exhausted and overwhelmed. Commit to excising that activity from your life as self-care; you deserve to use that time to focus on your fire.

HOW TO HOLD FIRM IN YOUR CONTROLLED BURN

Realizing things in your life need to change and being able to execute that change are two different things. Just as growing your fire will cause you and the people around you discomfort, eliminating things from your life will do the same. This discomfort can often prove extra challenging for women. Saying no doesn't come easy to most of us, and to conduct a controlled burn, you are going to have to say no and say no repeatedly.

It may be that you will have to say no to people in your life or walk away from a toxic job. Maybe like MILCK, you'll have to let go of the material things in your life that don't serve you—that also means you are saying no to the dreams or aspirations those material objects represented for you. It could be that you wanted to be thinner or wealthier or more popular—desires that are tied to the false fires we explored earlier in the book. Maybe letting go of material objects is a way for you to release one fire, like investing time in your art, for another, like getting involved with a local volunteer group. No matter what you are control-burning out of your life, it is sure to be a challenging but ultimately beneficial and rewarding process. These are some ways you can support yourself through this important step toward building your fire.

Start Small

Controlled burns work best when you slowly build them. Doing too much too soon can leave you feeling rash and off balance. Instead, focus on weeding out a few small things in your life that no longer serve you. Maybe you need to cut down on social media usage or you want to spend less time watching the news. As you test out what it feels like to eliminate these things, you'll realize that the natural next step makes itself apparent to you. If you successfully shrink the amount of news you watch, it won't be long before you find yourself asking your friends if you can try to limit your conversation about politics to no more than an hour a day.

Communicate Clearly

An effective controlled burn requires clear communication. When you decide to set a boundary with someone or if you decide to end a relationship, be direct and honest about your needs. Fall back on "I" statements to put the focus on your feelings and desires and to avoid accusing others. This is also a great time to lean on your values. Just as values add meaning to your desires, they bring weight and intention to the other choices you make in life. Practice these conversations with someone from your firestarter team.

Give Space to Your Emotions

Letting go of anything, whether it is a relationship or an old pair of jeans, stirs up emotions. As you work through your controlled burn, make sure to give yourself space for those feelings, especially if you are conducting a bigger controlled burn like ending a relationship or changing the way you interact with family. Before you embark on a controlled burn, make a plan for how you will care for yourself as these feelings arise. Can you treat yourself to a fun outing? Spend a morning journaling? Get together with the friends you call for emotional support?

Practice with Patience

Enforcing the boundaries that come with a controlled burn takes practice. Over time, you'll find that you can hold those boundaries more confidently and that you have a stronger connection to your own wants and needs, because that is ultimately what a controlled burn is all about. You don't conduct controlled burns to shut people out but to ensure that your needs are met and you have the space to grow into the best version of yourself. Remember, real self-care is not a onetime fix but a lifelong practice that allows you to protect your fire.

THE FLOWERS THAT BLOOM
FROM BURNOUT

Through her controlled burn, MILCK opened up the space to start her record label, Gentle Rebel Records, and her latest album includes a song about her experience of finding fame and then giving it back. It includes the lyric "You were a wildfire that burned it all away. I might have lost myself, but I found flowers in your place." By shifting her focus from all the things she was going to lose by starting over, MILCK could focus on what she had to gain, including a legacy she could be proud of when she looked back on her life. "I'm so grateful to get to this age and to be able to think about my legacy, which is such a weighted word," MILCK says. "But with the time I have left in my life, I want to focus on striking the right balance between caring for myself and giving to others."

The word "legacy" is often equated with big, extravagant gifts or accomplishments, like buildings named after wealthy donors or powerful companies. But your legacy isn't about your achievements—it's about paying attention to what gives your life meaning and giving others the permission to do the same. It's living in a way that assures you won't have regrets at the end of your life. In fact, the most common deathbed regret people have at the end of their lives is that they didn't live a life true to themselves. Living authentically, fully, and audaciously is a valuable legacy, and all women deserve the legacy of having made the most of their lives.

That perspective of limited time can crystallize what is imperative to your fulfillment and what debris can and should be burned away. For Landis Carey, the realization that she needed to completely reconfigure her life happened in a moment. One spring afternoon, Landis woke up from a nap in her bedroom and heard a voice say, "It's time to deal with this." The voice, which Landis recognized as her own, told her to move her hand to her abdomen and press down, where she felt a round, hard ball. Even though she had no symptoms of being sick, Landis made an appointment with her doctor. Soon after, an X-ray and other tests revealed a large tumor growing on her pancreas. Landis was just thirty-seven years old and the mother of three children under the age of six when she was diagnosed with cancer. She'd been working as a real estate agent in suburban New Jersey, where she and her husband were renovating a historic home. She thought she was fulfilled, but during her monthslong recovery from surgery to remove her tumor, Landis started questioning whether the life she'd created for herself and her family was what she really wanted. "I didn't want to go back to the life I'd been living, as if I was always climbing a mountain or running a race," Landis says. "I realized the only way forward was to leave everything I thought I wanted behind, including my job, my tennis club, my social life, my big home," Landis says.

As Landis methodically eliminated the things in her life that no longer served her, she found more space to move toward the things that sustained her, including a long-lost love of ceramics. When Landis was in her twenties, she'd turned down the opportunity to pursue her MFA in ceramics to go after more prestigious and lucrative jobs. When Landis was well enough, she got her pottery wheel out of storage and started throwing again. As time passed, the voice that had told Landis she was sick told her she should move her family from New Jersey to Florida to be closer to the ocean. Landis now lives in a beach town on the Atlantic and was recently granted a sought-after residency at an art center. She lives a simpler life, purposefully stripped down to what matters most: her family and her pottery. "Cancer unveiled illusion after illusion in my life, and I had to discard each one before I could move forward," Landis says. "So much had to be shed to get to this point—to finally pay attention to who I am and what I want—and those things are no longer negotiable."

PART FIVE

The Fire Cycle

On a breezy early summer afternoon in 2022, I found myself standing in the Rose Garden at the White House surrounded by dozens of other Moms Demand Action volunteers. We'd worked tirelessly for months to catalyze the nation's outrage into action after two horrific mass shooting tragedies—one in an elementary school in Uvalde, Texas, and one in a grocery store in Buffalo, New York. We'd held rallies and marches and met with our lawmakers. And now, unbelievably, the legislation that pundits said had a snowball's chance in hell of passing was becoming law, and we were at the White House with President Biden to celebrate.

After eleven years of demanding federal action on gun safety, we were incredulous and overjoyed that our hard work had finally paid off and we'd helped pass the first federal gun safety legislation through Congress in over a generation. And as I looked around at the dozens of women who had grown stronger, forged friendships, and fought for radical change in the face of harassment and threats—women who were now bonded as activists and friends for life—I could also see the impact I'd had by following my own fire so many years ago. And that's when I heard an inner voice say: "This is the end of this fire."

The words were an instruction I'd been waiting for for years. A few months after starting Moms Demand Action, a Silicon Valley volunteer who was working tirelessly to help me get the organization off the ground made an offhand comment at the end of one of our many daily phone calls. We discussed a reporter's request to interview me about my fledgling gun safety group. "Whatever you do," she said, "don't get founder's syndrome." I had no idea what that meant, but said, "Of course not," hung up, and Googled it. "Founder's syndrome" is how the tech world describes organizational founders whose identities become so enmeshed with their mission that it becomes almost impossible to untangle one from the other. And when those founders leave (either on their own accord or because they're forced out), the organizations fall apart.

At the time, I didn't know much about leading a nonprofit, but I knew I didn't want to develop founder's syndrome. As a practicing Buddhist, the last thing I wanted to do was to create an entire organization that would glorify me and not Moms Demand Action's mission. My goal was to tame my ego, not fuel it. So, I put a practice in place to maintain perspective: At the beginning of each year, I committed to asking myself whether it was time for me to step back and let another leader step forward. This wasn't just a simple exercise of asking myself if I should stay or go; I listed and contemplated all the reasons under the sun for both staying and leaving, and discussed them with my husband and confidants.

In the early years, my answer was almost always a firm "no." There was too much to do, and I still had a clear vision of what I wanted Moms Demand Action to accomplish and the energy to make it happen. But as the years went on, the answer to whether I should leave started leaning closer toward "maybe" or "yes," and I began to ponder my exit strategy. Invariably, though, a shooting tragedy or an urgent piece of legislation or an important election would change my mind, and I'd decide to stay.

But that afternoon, standing in the Rose Garden, I knew with total clarity that that celebration would be the bookend to my leadership and the beginning of a new chapter for Moms Demand Action. It was time for me to wind down the fire I'd started a decade ago—a fire that had grown beyond my wildest dreams, sparking fires in so many other women and creating a bonfire of women across the country.

16

Decay

After I realized it was time for me to step back from my leader-ship role at Moms Demand Action, I spent the next few months telling a handful of close confidants—women in my bonfire—about my decision. Some of those women had already moved on to other ventures themselves, and they gave me valuable advice about how to navigate the transition with integrity and authenticity. I used their input to plan my exit, including how to tell volunteers and in-troduce them to the next torchbearer. And then, because I knew it would be difficult to detach from the identity I'd cultivated and in-habited for over a decade, I created a personal plan to handle the in-evitable egoic suffering that would no doubt cause me to regret my decision. Just like there are traps we can fall into when we're grow-ing our fire, there are also traps we have to avoid when we're putting it out. I'd been at the helm of Moms Demand Action long enough to know that separating myself from my role would be fraught. Having worked in the corporate world, I'd seen too many leaders take a scorched-earth approach to leaving because their egos or identities were so tightly tied to what they'd built that they couldn't bear for it to carry on without them. My goal was to ensure that the organization lasted into perpetuity, and I reminded myself regularly that putting out my own fire was not, and should not be, the same as extinguishing the fire of Moms Demand Action.

That is not to say leaving wasn't difficult. During that year, there were plenty of times I felt angry at myself for deciding to leave, or I felt the sting of being on the sidelines while my team moved on without me, or I worried about who I would be or what I would do when I was done. But I'd like to think that because I'd planned for those uncomfortable moments, I was able to endure them. My husband and close friends held me accountable in the moments I reconsidered, and my therapist reminded me of all the reasons to be excited for the next chapter in my life. Most of all, I knew other women were watching me, and I wanted to be an example of what it looked like not just to lead, but to know when it was time to leave.

Knowing when it's time to put a fire out or to give it over to someone else to tend is a key tenet of living on fire. We discussed earlier in this book that too many women either decide not to start their fires or they put them out just as they begin to grow. But it's also possible to keep your fire burning for too long; to feel protective of your fire because it's yours, even when it no longer serves you. Here are some telltale signs that your fire is waning:

Stagnation: You've learned all you can and you've taught others everything you know.

Toxicity: Something that once brought out the best in you is now bringing out the worst.

Dread: You're actively looking for ways to avoid something you once enjoyed.

Boredom: What you've been doing no longer holds your interest, and you're ready for the next thing.

Intuition: Don't dismiss your gut; if you find yourself thinking more often about leaving than staying, trust what your inner voice is telling you.

New opportunities: Don't get so attached to one fire that you don't want another one. This is a cycle; always be scanning the horizon for what's next.

Looking back, Brooke Baldwin says she should have left her dream job at CNN much earlier. Things hadn't felt quite right for years, but she couldn't bring herself to move on from the fire she'd started thirteen years before. In the end, the network put Brooke's fire out for her; she was unceremoniously let go by management, and even though she knew it needed to happen, being asked to leave felt like a gut punch. Brooke had put so much of her talent and time into her career that it felt like a waste to walk away, even when that was what she truly wanted. "When I read my journals the years leading up to my leaving, I knew I needed to go," Brooke says. "But I'd made my career my top priority, over partners, friends, family, and everything else. I'd given so much to that place and to those people that I couldn't imagine doing anything else with my life."

With time to reflect, Brooke was able to reimagine her life, and she realized her job at CNN wasn't the only fire she'd kept going for too long; it was also time to leave her marriage and New York City. By moving on, Brooke could see that keeping fires going even when they no longer served her drained her desires and dimmed her spark. Not only had she sacrificed her fulfillment, but she had also missed out on a myriad of other opportunities that could have helped her figure out what she actually wanted to do with her life. "Leaving CNN was what helped me finally realize I had been out of alignment in many ways for many years," Brooke says. "I was so intricately linked with what I did for so long that it became who I was, and because it took me so long to leave, I had to do a lot of work on myself before I could start whatever came next."

It's only when you realize the strength of your flame is not measured by the success of any individual fire, but by your lifelong commitment to tending and growing many fires, that you can start to see the value and opportunity in ending a single fire. No sole fire can sustain you forever. And more likely than not, you will know when it is time to move on; you just have to listen. I've collected some ways to avoid waiting too long to put your fire out and move on.

DETERMINE WHAT IS ENOUGH

It's important to feel fulfilled, but how do you know when it's enough? If you're constantly comparing your fire to other people's, it might make you want to make your fire too big. Or if you set your expectations so high that you're unable to appreciate what you've achieved, you might try to make your fire last longer. But when you know going in what is enough, that becomes your signal that you've reached the end of your fire. At the outset of her career in basketball, Devereaux Peters made a pact with herself: She would never play past her prime. That's because Devereaux had seen what happened when other players refused to retire, despite minds and bodies that were no longer in the game. She committed to never doing that to herself or her team. "I knew that once I said I was done with basketball, I was going to be done for good," Devereaux says. "I wasn't going to take other people's opportunities away just because I didn't know what to do with myself after retirement."

After Devereaux had played basketball for teams in America and overseas for over seven years, she woke up one morning in France and had a feeling she'd never had in her entire career: She didn't want to go to practice. Lying in bed, she realized this was the signal she'd prepared herself for since the beginning of her career. "This has been a great run, but I'm done," she realized. With that, the two-time WNBA champion called her coach and retired. Devereaux waited to share her decision publicly so no one would try to talk her out of it, and by the time the public did find out, Devereaux had already moved on in her mind. However, she had only ever played basketball as a job; not knowing what was next was nerve-racking and it took her months to get her footing. But, because she was proud of herself for keeping her commitment to go when it was time, she never doubted her decision. "I haven't touched a basketball since and I don't miss playing at all," Devereaux says. "There are a lot of athletes who miss the game and are unable to move on, but I feel like I did everything I needed to do."

The challenge to knowing when it's time to walk away from

your fire is to start with the awareness that, one way or another, you will eventually need to go. Whether you make a pact with yourself like Devereaux did or ask the women on your firestarter team to keep you in check, find a way to honestly assess whether the passion and vision for your fire have faded. And remember that even when one fire dies out, your spark is still with you, ready to ignite your next fire.

LIGHT THE MATCH

How will you know when your fire is enough?

In your firestarter journal, imagine the milestones that will mark the end of your fire. Write down your definition of success. What is enough money, fame, recognition, friends? What boundaries or goals will signal to you that you've done enough or are ready to move on?

PRESERVE WHAT YOU'VE BUILT

The human ego is a funny and fragile thing—it can be difficult to walk away from people, places, and ideas that we are attached to, especially when we feel like we played a role in creating or bettering them. So when you realize it's time to move on from a fire you started, it might be tempting to put that fire out not just for yourself but for everyone else who's getting warmth from it, too. It's the "If I can't have it, no one else can either" mentality. We've all seen this scenario play out in real life, especially in the corporate world. A

leader is asked or decides to step aside, but because they're operating from a place of ego, they're unable to do so with grace. They
might subconsciously undermine the team that takes over for them
by talking about them negatively in public or private. They might
refuse to hand over the reins totally to their successor and usurp
their authority by continuing to act as the leader. Or they might decide to compete against the team they're leaving.

These impulses are normal and human, but acting on them is
unproductive and can even damage your reputation. Certainly,
there were things that didn't sit quite right with me during my time
as a leader in the gun safety movement—not just working for free for
over a decade, but also several incidences of sexism and bullying.
But while exposing those injustices or calling those people out publicly might make me feel better personally, it wouldn't help anyone
else—in fact, it would be harmful if my actions ended up weakening
the movement for my own satisfaction. That's why it's important to
keep the original intention behind your fire at the front of your
mind, especially when it's time to walk away. Remember that every
fire becomes part of your legacy. It deserves to live on—if not for
you, then for others.

LIGHT THE MATCH

Keep your ego in check

Like my plan to manage my negative emotions around stepping back from Moms Demand Action, create your own list
of all the ways your ego might interfere with your decision
to put out your fire. What steps should you consider taking

to prevent that from happening? Now share that list with a close confidant—someone you trust—and ask them to help you stay on track.

LET YOUR NEXT FIRE FIND YOU

The phrase "letting the game come to you" encapsulates an approach in sports that encourages athletes to be patient and disciplined, rather than trying too hard to make plays that might backfire. This same approach can be applied to letting your fire die out and finding a new one; it's the ability to tolerate discomfort and uncertainty while having the presence of mind to bear witness to whatever unfolds instead of forcing it. This doesn't mean you should wait for new fires to start, but that you should give yourself time to explore new fires and allow new opportunities to present themselves.

When Zerlina Maxwell got the call telling her the MSNBC newscast she'd anchored for two years was going to be canceled, she was asked to think about whether she was willing to stay on at the cable channel, but in a different capacity. After giving it a lot of thought, Zerlina made the monumental decision to walk away from the network and start over, even though she had no idea what she wanted to do next. But she knew jumping into another job without creating the space to figure out what she wanted would backfire. "At some point, everyone needs to move on, and that's what I chose to do," Zerlina says. "I was presented with the rare opportunity to make an intentional choice to find and do things in my life that would light me up, something my job on television no longer did."

Even though Zerlina's manager kept calling her to try to pin her down on next steps, she spent her new free time focusing on more creative pursuits, including learning how to golf, traveling abroad, and doing a deep dive into K-pop. Zerlina also leaned into hosting her political call-in radio show on SiriusXM, which had been a part-time gig while she worked at MSNBC. The more Zerlina invested in that show, the more she realized how much she valued the interaction with her audience, something she didn't have on television. "I'm in transition, and I'm allowing the universe to show me what's next," Zerlina says.

It's a courageous act of self-awareness and self-love to recognize when it's time to move on, to let go of what's familiar or comfortable, and to open ourselves up to new possibilities. And when you reach the end of one fire, you'll gain profound perspectives about how it transformed you, and you'll use that knowledge to take on whatever fire is next. Endings are never the end, just a necessary component of this lifelong practice of rebirth; to allow your fire to change form, you have to be willing to let old versions of yourself burn away.

FAN THE FLAMES

Get guidance on self-care

Reach out to your firestarter team and ask what they've done in their downtime to restore themselves during periods between fires and then commit to trying a few of their recommendations. If you're looking for inspiration, start with some of the ideas below.

- Explore new places, even if it's just a new corner of your neighborhood.

- Think of the most pointless way to spend an afternoon and do it.

- Commit to a specific period of nothingness, whether it's a week, month, or year, and tell the people in your life that you're preparing for whatever is next.

Winding your fire down is not a sign of failure but a vital process that allows for renewal and growth. Recognizing that it's time to let a fire die out makes space for fresh beginnings. Just as no fire can burn forever, our personal and professional pursuits also need to end to make room for new opportunities. Embrace the end of a fire with the understanding that it paves the way for future endeavors, ensuring continuous growth and transformation. By accepting and planning for this decay, you create a legacy that lives on and fuels the next chapter of your journey.

Conclusion

Rebirth

The first sign of life after a fire in a forest is a wildflower, aptly named fireweed. Also called the phoenix of flowers, these tall, steadfast wild plants with pink and purple blooms grow and thrive in the new soil and sunlight created in the wake of forest fires. When they bloom, it signals to the rest of nature that it's time for a resurgence. As other plants follow the fireweed's lead and fill in the areas that have been burned away, the fireweed dies back but leaves its seeds in the soil so that after the next fire, its blooms can start the cycle all over again. Like fireweed, you, too, will rise from the ashes of who you were before you started your fire and bloom into a new version of yourself. As a firestarter, this is the same cycle your fires will follow: growth, decay, and then rebirth and renewal.

And like the fireweed, it is important to take space between fires. To reflect on what you've learned or accomplished, to rest and recover, and to move forward with a renewed sense of energy so you're not wasting time starting fires you don't want or need just because you're afraid of the important pause that needs to take place between fires. Living on fire is all about living in alignment with your innermost desires. Your ability to act authentically on those desires is tested every time you ignite, grow, and sustain a fire, but your ability to listen to those desires is tested most when you are in the time between fires. After Sandy Weicher was laid off from her corporate job of thirty years, a career she was deeply passionate about, she found herself having an identity crisis in her sixties. Who was she if not a busy executive? "I felt stuck and lost," Sandy says. "But early on, I got some good advice from someone who said, 'Don't do anything for a year.'"

Sandy followed that counsel and began working with a therapist who helped her reframe her firing as a new life chapter that would allow her to explore who she was and what she wanted. She knew she needed to start that exploration by getting acclimated to a slower pace of life and detaching from the busyness that had fueled her. Soon, Sandy was taking daily meditative walks in Central Park, working on jigsaw puzzles, and practicing pickleball. Slowly but surely, Sandy stopped jonesing for conference calls and started looking forward to activities that had nothing to do with her former job. "At first, the pace was maddening, and I wanted so badly to jump into the next big thing," Sandy says. "But I needed the downtime and space, and to get comfortable with the discomfort that came with slowing down, before I could move on."

By the end of her year off, Sandy knew what she wanted to do next, and it married her values, abilities, and desires—all the elements of her fire triangle. As a former business coach, Sandy valued teaching and mentoring, and as a cancer survivor, she had a passion for educating other people about how to navigate the disease. Sandy took all the learnings from the first half of her life and transitioned them into the next half by creating a national support group for bladder cancer survivors. "I'm proud of what I accomplished during my decades-long career, but the time I took to decide what was next helped me see it was time to try something completely different."

Seeing clearly who we are based on the patterns of our life is one of the great privileges of getting older, and it's why living on fire is just as important during the second half of our lives as it is in the first. And maybe it's an advantage. When you're young, you wonder who you'll become, but by the time you're middle-aged, you know who you are—you just have to allow yourself to be her. When Maria Shriver was young, she thought she knew what the story of her life would be: She was a renowned journalist at CBS and NBC, she was the wife of an actor, she was the daughter of two philanthropists, and she was the mother of four children—those were the identities that kept her moored. But then, several events in Maria's life forced her to change course completely. First, her husband decided to run for governor of California, and she was unexpectedly fired very publicly (and by fax). Later, within a span of two years, Maria's parents passed away and her relationship with her husband of twenty-five years ended in a high-profile divorce. "With each life crisis, there was an 'end of the world' feeling, like the ground wouldn't stop shifting," Maria says. "At the time, it felt like one disaster after another."

After each lifequake, Maria gave herself permission to discover (or rediscover) what would come next. Instead of forcing it, she trusted that her values, abilities, and burning desires would lead her to the next thing. And now, at age sixty-eight, Maria doesn't view those transitional events in her life as disasters, but as learning experiences that led her to be the real her—the person she was meant to be. "I feel like I'm right where I should be, and now I can see that all my work has laddered upon laddered upon laddered right up to this very moment and that everything that I've ever worked on has brought me to this place," Maria says. "No matter what happens in your life—if you're fired, your marriage blows up, someone dies—whenever you find yourself in unfamiliar territory, remember that this is just the beginning of a new version of who you will become."

During my last year leading Moms Demand Action, in addition to saying my goodbyes, I slowly started to detach myself from the work. I limited my hours and handed projects and opportunities over to other team members. I signed up for a weeklong retreat with a group of strangers and got vulnerable about the transition I was going through. I started seeing a therapist trained in psychedelics and went on a twelve-hour journey to unearth the emotions, including vicarious trauma, that were stuck in my subconscious. I got back to my love of writing from childhood and started writing essays on Substack. I used my social media platforms to focus on things other than gun violence, like women's issues. And then, after realizing that I had neglected my friendships during my tenure at Moms Demand Action (the irony is not lost on me), at age fifty, I set out to make new friends.

During that year, I made a concerted effort to shift the focus of my energy, to rest when I could, and to think about what I wanted to do, if I wanted to do anything at all, next. Toward the end of that year, I got an unexpected call from Maria Shriver. I didn't know Maria well, but she'd used her platform to promote gun safety activism and Moms Demand Action, and I respected her immensely.

Maria was calling with a proposition: write a book for her publishing imprint about what I'd learned through my activism about women and leadership. I took a few weeks to think about Maria's offer, and the more I considered it, the more it felt like it was lighting up all the elements of my fire triangle. During my activism, I realized that it wasn't just gun safety that I was passionate about; more than anything else, it was helping women summon their audacity.

This is the fierce clarity that can come from living on fire; it brings your life into focus by asking you to look at whether you're living by your values, honoring your abilities, or if you're actually hiding away your most profound desires and aspirations. It requires you to decide if you're willing and able to unearth what you want and to recognize if you're actively thwarting your own fulfillment. It demands that you stop sabotaging the things that would bring you the most satisfaction by telling yourself, "I can't now, I'm too busy, it won't work, I have to, I can't." And it confronts you with the questions "What are you waiting for? If not now, when?"

As someone who often sits with people who are dying, Rabbi Sharon Brous has seen that humans often only have insight about who they are and what they want when they're nearing or think they are nearing the end of their life—when there's too little time to do those things. After Rabbi Brous's friend, a young mother, died from breast cancer, she decided to use the high holy days to have her congregation reflect on why they defer their fulfillment. Rabbi Brous handed out a stack of index cards and Sharpies to hundreds of her parishioners and told them to answer the question, "What are you waiting for to do what you want with your life?" That night, she wept at her dinner table as she went through the answers on the cards. People said they were waiting for someone to tell them they're beautiful, for their parents to love them, for someone to tell them to write the book, to start the band, to tell them that they're worthy of love.[1] "I just thought, 'My God, you're not waiting for someone else to say that to you, you're actually waiting to feel it yourself,'" Rabbi Brous says. "We have to give ourselves permission to live as if we could be dead tomorrow, and this is especially challenging for women because we're taught to put our dreams on the back burner while we take care of everyone else's."

During the first half of women's lives, we're often so focused on building our lives with a focus on helping and supporting others that we forget our time is finite. But when we reach midlife, we finally have the wisdom to see that we hold the power to burn it all down and build new lives focused on what *we* want. If you take one thing from this book, let it be this: You are allowed—even obligated—to decide how to live your life. And it is never too late to decide to live your life on fire. At almost seventy years old, Sandra Cisneros, the poet and author who writes about the freedom that comes from becoming an older woman, is still looking for her next fire while also preparing for the end of her life, a transformative period that is fueling her creativity. "It's like everything in my life has brought me up to this stage," Sandra says. "I still have a lot to learn, and I haven't written the book I want to be known for, but I'm getting closer with every book I write. I'm in this magical phase of my life that everything has been leading up to. I don't know how much time I have, and I don't want to waste any of it."

Acknowledging the finiteness of our lives can be an important wake-up call, no matter how young or old you are. Life is short and time is precious—*your time* is precious. You deserve to live so that when you get to the end of your life, you know you were fully alive. That every time you were given the opportunity to choose between your desire and obligation, you chose the fiery thing. That your legacy is a life on fire.

Rebirth is both the end and the beginning of the fire cycle. This is where you rise from the ashes of your past endeavors, carrying the wisdom and experiences you've gained along the way. Every new first isn't just a fresh venture—it's a continuation of your journey, enriched by the lessons and support you've gathered along the way. Every time you rise from the ashes, you do so as a wiser, stronger, more capable firestarter. To live on fire is a radical act of self-love and defiance in a world that often asks women to snuff out their flames. The stories, tools, and lessons in this book are not just about finding your fire but about sustaining it, protecting it, sharing it, and rebuilding it time and time again until you've built a life that is so unequivocally ablaze it lights a path for others. This cycle of growth, decay, and rebirth is the essence of living on fire.

By the time my last day as the leader of Moms Demand Action rolled around on New Year's Eve of 2023, I was at home in California with my husband, and our plan was to celebrate the New Year with a glass of champagne and then to be in bed long before midnight. But as the day went on, I felt the need to mark the end of an era. I was yearning for some kind of ritual that helped me honor the fire I was ending and to create space for the next fire, writing this book. My husband had lit a candle on our dinner table, and that's when I realized I needed a fire ceremony—something practiced for generations among Indigenous people to let go of the past and step into the future, and now, they're commonplace across religions and cultures to encourage healing, honor rites of passage, and mark key events, and, coincidentally, they often take place around the New Year.

At twilight, I wrapped myself in a blanket, took the candle from the table, and walked outside. I wandered around the backyard for a bit, trying to determine the best place for my fire ceremony. I finally sat down in the grass under the canopy of one of the scraggly, sprawling California oaks in our backyard. I held the candle up and stared into its tiny flame. I thanked the fire for transforming my life and giving me new life. And then, after I blew out its flame, I watched the white smoke swirl and dance into the darkening sky.

LIGHT THE MATCH

Ponder the finiteness of time

Many of us live life as though our time on earth is infinite, so imagine that you're told you have only one year left to live. In your firestarter journal, write down ten things you'd stop doing and ten things you would do. Now write about why you're not doing those things and how you can begin to move toward the life you'd live if you knew when it was ending.

FAN THE FLAMES

Hold your own fire ceremony

Rituals help us show gratitude for what we've experienced, to acknowledge and let go of what no longer serves us, to set intentions for the future, and to make space for what's to come in our lives. There are many different ways to honor the fire inside you, as well as a fire you'd like to end or begin, but start by reenacting your own mini fire ceremony using a candle. Purposefully light its flame as a symbol of your own fire and meditate on the flame as you consider what you're ready to let go of and what you want to begin. And when you blow out the flame, watch the smoke until it ends, imagining it represents your intentions.

Acknowledgments

To every woman in my life who encouraged or helped me start and grow my own fires, thank you. This book is the culmination of the lessons I've learned because of the lessons you were willing to share. Your belief in me, your wisdom, and your strength are the sparks that kept me going, even on the hardest days.

To every Moms Demand Action volunteer who was willing to follow me into battle and listen when I told them that they, too, needed to grow their fires—this book would not exist without you. Together, we built a movement fueled by love, determination, and the unrelenting belief in a safer future. You are my endless inspiration.

A special thanks is owed to Glennon Doyle, who helped me shape the narrative for this book and for showing me that my anger is really fire that can illuminate the way forward.

To Sarah Hartley, Lisa Hazen, Elizabeth Gassman, and Emily Lavelle, thank you for your dedication, your expertise, and your commitment to this book. You made the process not just possible but deeply rewarding. I could not have asked for a better team.

To Maria Shriver, thank you for believing in this book before I did. Your invitation to write about women and their inherent power has proven to be my most exciting fire yet. I'm also indebted to Cassidy Graham for her keen editorial eye. Thank you to Lynn Buckley for designing a beautiful cover, to Claire Vaccaro and Daniel Lagin for making the interior shine, to Nick Michal and Anna Dobbin for keeping the production of this book effortless and orderly. I'm grateful to the entire team at The Open Field and Penguin Random House for doing all they can to share my work with readers.

Thank you to my literary agent, the inimitable Mollie Glick.

To all the women who shared their stories with me, whether in an interview, a direct message online, or a quick conversation at a party, your courage and vulnerability are the beating heart of this book. And to everyone who joined our Playing with Fire conversations on Substack, which brought this book to life—thank you for your time, insight, and passion.

To this extraordinary group of firestarters—your wisdom, kindness, and leadership inspire me every single day: A'shanti Gholar, Aliza Pressman, Amanda Doyle, Amanda Haas, Amber Goodwin, Amy Diehl, Andrea Hunley, Anna King, Annie Andrews, Anushay Hossain, Ayelet Waldman, Becca Moyer Defelice, Bridgette Sloan, Brooke Baldwin, Caitlin Crosby, Charlotte Clymer, Danielle Mai, Devereaux Peters, Eve Levenson, Eve Rodsky, Geri Jannarone, Gisele Barreto Fetterman, Gretchen Carlson, Jennifer Boylan, Jennifer Herrera, Jennifer Louden, Jennifer Siebel Newsom, Jerri Green, Jessica Yellin, Jo Ella Hoye, Julia Boorstin, Julie Bogart, Kelly Peters, Kirsten Powers, Kristin Neff, Landis Carey, Lisa Ling,

ACKNOWLEDGMENTS

Lisa Sun, Lucy McBath, Mallory McMorrow, Mandana Dayani, Margo Price, Melissa Wiley, Michelle Sinnott, Mika Brzezinski, MILCK (Connie Lim), Mimi Rocah, Monica Molenaar, Nazanin Boniadi, Ny Whitaker, Olivia Julianna, Pamela Ebstyne King, Pooja Lakshmin, Quiana Agbai, Rebecca Bauer-Kahan, Rennae Stubbs, Samara Bay, Sandra Cisneros, Sara Smirin, Sharon Brous, Sharon Salzberg, Sonni Mun, Stephanie Lundy, Stephanie Ruhle, Stephannie Lane Baker, Susan McPherson, Susan Piver, Tara Mohr, Zerlina Maxwell, and Zoe Winkler Reinis.

Finally, to my husband, John, and our children—Kelly, Samantha, Abby, Remy, and Sam—thank you for always encouraging me to find and follow my fire.

Notes

CHAPTER 1: WHAT IT MEANS TO LIVE ON FIRE

1. "Louise Slaughter (1929–2018)," University of Rochester, May 26, 2020, https://www.rochester.edu/2020-celebration/louise-slaughter.

CHAPTER 2: WHAT YOUR FIRE IS NOT

1. Kate Bowler, "Liz Gilbert: Why Your Creativity Matters," *Everything Happens with Kate Bowler*, Lemonada, December 14, 2022, https://podcasts.apple.com/us/podcast/liz-gilbert-why-your-creativity-matters/id1341076079?i=1000624691338.
2. Arthur C. Brooks and Oprah Winfrey, *Build the Life You Want: The Art and Science of Getting Happier* (New York: Portfolio, 2023), 5.

CHAPTER 3: WHY WOMEN DON'T LIVE ON FIRE AND WHY YOU MUST ANYWAY

1. Dina Gerdeman, "Want to Be Happier? Make More Free Time," *Harvard Business School Working Knowledge*, July 10, 2018, https://hbswk.hbs.edu/item/want-to-be-happier-make-more-free-time.
2. Oliver Lewis, "Women More Likely to Suffer from Imposter Syndrome Than Men, According to Research," *The Independent*, April 7, 2023, https://www.independent.co.uk/life-style/women-imposter-syndrome-workplace-confidence-b2313770.html.

CHAPTER 5: FINDING THE HEAT OF YOUR DESIRES

1. Joan Wylie Hall, ed., *Conversations with Audre Lorde* (Jackson: University Press of Mississippi, 2004), 91.

NOTES

CHAPTER 6: TAPPING INTO THE OXYGEN OF YOUR VALUES

1. Brené Brown, *Dare to Lead: Brave Work. Tough Conversations. Whole Hearts* (New York: Random House, 2018), 188.
2. "Michigan Lawmaker's Forceful Speech Rebuts 'Grooming' Attack," NBC News, April 21, 2022, https://www.nbcnews.com/nbc-out/out-politics-and-policy/michigan-lawmakers-forceful-speech-rebuts-grooming-attack-rcna25365.

CHAPTER 9: KEEPING THE FLAMES ALIVE

1. Brené Brown, "Brené on Day 2," *Dare to Lead with Brené Brown* (podcast), September 2, 2020, https://brenebrown.com/podcast/brene-on-day-2.

CHAPTER 10: TOOLS TO SUSTAIN YOUR FIRE

1. Carol S. Dweck, *Mindset: The New Psychology of Success* (New York: Random House, 2006).

CHAPTER 11: BONFIRE

1. "The Scandalous Origins of Gossip," Unbabel, December 10, 2019, https://unbabel.com/the-scandalous-origins-of-gossip.

CHAPTER 13: THE TRAPS EXTINGUISHERS CREATE

1. Glennon Doyle, *Untamed* (New York: Dial Press, 2020), 75.
2. Donald J. Trump (@realDonaldTrump), "I heard poorly rated @Morning_Joe speaks badly of me (don't watch anymore). Then how come low I.Q. Crazy Mika, along with Psycho Joe, came..," Twitter (now X), June 29, 2017, https://x.com/realDonaldTrump/status/880408582310776832.
3. Donald J. Trump (@realDonaldTrump), ". . . to Mar-a-Lago 3 nights in a row around New Year's Eve, and insisted on joining me. She was bleeding badly from a face-lift. I said no!," Twitter (now X), June 29, 2017, https://twitter.com/realDonaldTrump/status/880410114456465411.

CONCLUSION: REBIRTH

1. Sharon Brous, *The Amen Effect: Ancient Wisdom to Mend Our Broken Hearts and World* (New York: Avery, 2024), 70–72.